#1 *NEW YORK TIMES* BESTSELLING AUTHOR

MIKE EVANS

THE
VISIONARIES

P.O. BOX 30000, PHOENIX, AZ 85046

The Visionaries

Copyright © 2017 All rights reserved Printed in the United States of America

Published by TimeWorthy Books Phoenix, AZ 85046

Hardcover:978-1-62961-125-9
Paperback:978-1-62961-126-6
Canada:978-1-62961-127-3

*For the vision **is** yet for an appointed time;*
But at the end it will speak, and it will not lie.
Though it tarries, wait for it;
Because it will surely come, It will not tarry.
(Habakkuk 2:3)

FOREWORD 7

HORATIO GATES SPAFFORD
Chapter 1 11
Chapter 2 23
Chapter 3 37

LAURENCE OLIPHANT
Chapter 1 49
Chapter 2 59
Chapter 3 71

WILLIAM BLACKSTONE
Chapter 1 83
Chapter 2 91
Chapter 3 101

WILLIAM HECHLER
Chapter 1 111
Chapter 2 123
Chapter 3 131

ARTHUR BALFOUR
Chapter 1 139
Chapter 2 147
Chapter 3 155

DAVID LLOYD GEORGE
Chapter 1 163
Chapter 2 173
Chapter 3 181

WALTER CLAY LOWDERMILK
Chapter 1 191
Chapter 2 199
Chapter 3 207

THEODOR HERZL
Chapter 1 215
Chapter 2 223
Chapter 3 229

DAVID BEN-GURION
Chapter 1 239
Chapter 2 249
Chapter 3 259

LORD ANTHONY ASHLEY-COOPER
Chapter 1 267
Chapter 2 273
Chapter 3 279

AFTERWORD 295

FOREWORD

A visionary is someone who can envision what the future *could* be, but the dream or vision doesn't end there. The culmination requires labor and tenacity. King Solomon wrote in Proverbs 29:18, "Where there is no vision, the people perish."

The prophet Isaiah foresaw the rebirth of the Nation of Israel. *The Message* records the event this way:

> Before she went into labor, she had the baby.
> Before the birth pangs hit, she delivered a son.
> Has anyone ever heard of such a thing? Has any-
> one seen anything like this? A country born in a
> day? A nation born in a flash? But Zion was barely
> in labor when she had her babies! (Isaiah 66:7-8)

On May 14, 1948, after almost 2,900 years, the Jewish people reclaimed their homeland. During a day's time—24 hours—the Nation of Israel was miraculously reborn.

The United Nations had issued a mandate, the British had withdrawn, gentile control of the land had ceased, and Isaiah's prophecy had come to fruition.

God gave the prophet Habakkuk a vision of redemption:

> For the vision *is* yet for an appointed time;
> But at the end it will speak, and it will not lie.
> Though it tarries, wait for it; because it will
> surely come, it will not tarry. (Habakkuk 2:3)

In the 1800s, long before the events of 1948, a cause—Zionism—was born. It set the stage; it attracted the men and women who would be instrumental in the rebirth of Israel. They had caught the vision of God's plan to restore His Chosen People to their homeland. Added to the list of ardent visionaries were men such as Lord Shaftesbury, Spafford, Oliphant, Blackstone, Hechler, Balfour, Lloyd-George, Herzl, and Ben-Gurion.

The culmination of their vision was realized in 1948. Since that momentous date, Israel has had to fight for her life—not once but multiple times. Joining the Jewish people in the trenches were sympathetic gentiles from around the world. With each succeeding battle for existence, new Christian Zionist organizations have sprung up to stand with the Children of Israel in their battle to survive.

This book tells the stories of the men who staunchly supported the Jewish people before and during the formation of the State of Israel.

HORATIO GATES
SPAFFORD

When peace, like a river, attendeth my way,
When sorrows like sea billows roll;
Whatever my lot, Thou has taught me to say,
It is well, it is well, with my soul.

—HORATIO SPAFFORD

1

The elder Horatio Gates Spafford was born February 18, 1778 in Vermont. The squalling little boy made his appearance just four months after British General John Burgoyne surrendered to Colonial General Horatio Gates. It was a pivotal moment for the emerging nation, and Captain John Spafford, a veteran of the wars for independence insisted on naming his newborn son after the illustrious General Gates.

Spafford, Sr. was a most unusual man—writer, inventor, farmer, and vociferous advocate of democracy. He was an avid self-promoter who shared his thoughts and ideas with some of the most well-known men of his day, i.e., lawyer and statesman John Adams; author of the Declaration of Independence Thomas Jefferson; lexicographer Noah

Webster; and Massachusetts Representative Josiah Quincy. As an inventor, he was granted a patent for an upgraded fireplace—a move that began a long-term struggle to improve the process for gaining a patent and the laws that governed it. His labors to gain the patent led to a meeting with then-President James Madison.

Spafford, Sr. married Hannah Bristol with whom he sired six children. The two divorced on grounds of infidelity, and he later married Elizabeth Clark Hewitt. The couple had five additional offspring, the youngest of whom was Horatio Gates Spafford.

Horatio was four when his father died in 1932. A line from the elder Spafford's obituary reads as follows:

> In the death of Dr. Spafford, an interesting, but now deeply afflicted family has sustained an irreparable loss, and a large circle of friends will mourn his departure.[1]

Although his father was often thought to be bereft of cash and in fiscal hardship, young Horatio seemed to possess many benefits usually appreciated by those who enjoyed prosperity and prestige. He was an excellent student who easily captured scholarship awards and intellectual accolades. He was fascinated by the night sky that always seemed to him to be shrouded in a cloudy haze. Sitting with some friends one evening and listening to them exclaim about the brightness of the stars, he asked, "Do you really see enough beauty up there to warrant your outburst?"[2] His friends were flabbergasted by his question until one young man offered Horatio his eyeglasses. When he donned them, Horatio realized what he had missed as he sat mesmerized by the sparkling sky above him. So stunned was he by what he had seen that he later wrote the poem, "Night," the first stanza of which proclaimed his astonishment:

> Ye countless stars that tremble in the sky,
> How bright and beautiful are you tonight!
> I've known ye long, but never did my eye
> So burn beneath the glory of your light
> As it doth now; I kneel to ye—ye wear
> The impress of the Diety that's there.[3]

The discovery that he was nearsighted and the addition of spectacles changed Horatio's life in many ways, among them: He became much more outgoing, erudite, and insatiably inquisitive. He enrolled in law school, and after graduation moved to Chicago, the burgeoning city on Lake Michigan. There, he became active in the political scene. He was passionately against slavery, and supported

President Abraham Lincoln's stance following the Civil War, a detail he would share during rallies and get-togethers with family and friends. Captivated by science, Horatio became a professor of jurisprudence at Lind University, the division that later became the Feinberg School of Medicine at Northwestern University.

As a successful, vigorous, and unattached young man, he was besieged by Chicago mamas as a potential match for their unmarried daughters. He often had to run the gauntlet of those eager mothers just to exit his local Presbyterian Church where he taught a class for young girls. On one particular Sunday morning, he managed to escape the zealous matriarchs only to find himself the target of Cupid's arrow. As he left the sanctuary, he met Anna Larssen (Americanized to Lawson), the young woman who would become the love of his life and his wife.

Anna had been born in Stavanger, Norway in 1842 as Anne Tobine Larsdatter Oglende. In May 1846, Bjarne Lars Larssen Oglende, his wife Gurine, and four-year old daughter Anne set sail for New York on the *Norden*. Lars had left behind his two children from a previous marriage, Edward and Rachel, who would later join him in the States. After arriving in the United States, they set a course for Chicago where the family would settle. Not only had they left Norway behind, the family soon abandoned their strange Norwegian names for less unwieldy ones. Bjarne became Lars; Gurine adopted the name Tanetta, and Anne became simply Anna.

The city of Chicago boasted wooden buildings, bridges, and even elevated sidewalks constructed to keep its citizens above the mud in the winter and dust in the summer. This practice contributed greatly to the fire hazard in the city. That was not the only danger in nineteenth century Chicago:

> Lake Michigan's swampy shore bred mosquitos, so malaria, or "ague fever," as it was called, swept the city at regular intervals. The Chicago River was an open sewer, and while steps were already being taken to ensure a clean water supply by driving a pipeline deep into Lake Michigan, there were also periodic outbreaks of scarlet fever, diphtheria, smallpox, typhoid, and cholera.[4]

The city had suffered an epidemic of cholera in 1832, one that had been spread by immigrants arriving in British ships. It spread from New York to Chicago, claiming the lives of hundreds. The devastating plague spurred the foundation of the Chicago Board of Health to combat communicable diseases, resulting in the founding of several orphanages to care for children left behind after their families were ravaged by illness and death.

A resurgence of the disease in 1849 profoundly affected Anna and her half-siblings. Cholera claimed the life of her mother, Tanetta, and baby brother, Hans. Anna, her father, Lars, Rachel, and Edward, survived. For six years the family struggled to keep body and soul together—until Lars began to feel the effects of a recurrence of tuberculosis. He had heard that the cold, hard winters in Minnesota would kill germs, so in a desperate attempt to cure his illness, Lars and Edward departed Chicago for Minnesota. Anna was left behind with neighbor Sarah Ely where she thrived, both on Mrs. Ely's kindness and education at the highly-acclaimed Dearborn Academy. Just before her fourteenth birthday, Anna was notified that her father had suffered a recurrence of tuberculosis. She left Chicago for the wilds of southeast Minnesota near the beginning of winter in 1856. There in a half-finished log house, she found Edward and a very ill Lars.

While Goodhue County offered little in the way of safety for the young pioneer, Anna quickly took up the reins of homesteader as washwoman, cook, farmer, rancher, seamstress, and nurse. She had gone from city girl to frontier caretaker in a matter of weeks. Her first winter in Minnesota was one of the worst on record with temperatures often plunging below zero and wind-driven blizzards obscuring the landscape. Despite her unfailing efforts, her father died just before spring, leaving Anna and Edward to fend for themselves. Their nearest neighbor was seven long miles away, but many gathered to aid the two teens in burying their father. A coffin was fashioned from pieces of wood, lined with straw and a sheet from the cabin, and then covered with fragrant boughs of fir. After the funeral, Edward drove his sister to a farm where a circuit-riding preacher was staying. Anna planned to accompany him to Red Wing where she could connect to a train bound for Chicago.

Edward dropped her at the farm, turned the wagon around and headed home. Anna, with tears cascading down her face, ran alongside the wagon as long as she could. She had vowed never to return to Minnesota, a pledge that would mean her last glimpse of Edward was sitting on the wagon seat headed back to the farm he had inherited from his father.

After several weeks of waiting for the preacher to complete his rounds and accompany her, Anna finally returned to Chicago to live with her half-sister, Rachel Frederickson. At Dearborn she resumed her voice and music instruction, and was quickly recognized as a stellar student. At the age of fifteen and after the harsh winter in the wilds of Minnesota, Anna was more mature than most girls her age. A friend described her as having "the bluest eyes, and abundant fair hair, with beautifully molded mouth and chin, and very white and even teeth . . . . She had a merry, kind, and affectionate disposition that won the hearts of many people . . . . Her voice was lovely, and people predicted that when it was trained, a great future lay before her."[5]

When Horatio laid eyes on Anna, he was quickly smitten. By the time she and Horatio met, unbeknownst to him she was only fifteen; he was twenty-nine. After courting the lovely young lady for a year, he was shocked to learn that the accomplished young woman was only sixteen, too young for marriage. Horatio sat down with Anna and her sister and arranged for his intended to attend The Ferry Institute for Young Ladies outside Chicago. Anna wrote to her long-time friend, Mrs. Ely:

> I wish you were acquainted with Mr. Spafford. He is a true and noble man. I owe him a great deal, but still I would not marry him merely from gratitude.[6]

When Anna reached her nineteenth birthday, the couple married in Second Presbyterian Church on September 5,

1861. They made their home in Lake View, a suburb of Chicago where they frequently entertained overnight guests and sometimes financially supported them as well. Horatio had been active in the abolitionist crusade and their cottage was a meeting place for activists in the reform movements of the time. This included crusaders such as Frances E. Willard, National Women's Christian Temperance Union president, and several Evangelical leaders.

The decade following the Spafford union produced four daughters: Anna, Margaret, Elizabeth, and Tanetta. Horatio had become a successful and respected lawyer, but felt dissatisfied, as if something were missing from his life. Standing on the courthouse steps one day during lunch, he heard dynamic shoe-salesman-turned-evangelist, Dwight L. Moody preach on repentance. There was nothing about Moody that commanded attention and yet Horatio could not take his eyes off the stocky man.

Day after day, Spafford returned to hear the evangelist preach the gospel; night after night, he pondered the challenging words he had heard that noon. Finally, he asked God to show him the abundant life in Christ espoused by Moody. Horatio's life was forever changed as he joined with others who prayed daily for spiritual change in Chicago. He held meetings in the local jails, visited the sick in the city's hospitals, and invested his own funds in outreach—both compassionate and evangelistic. Horatio united with other businessmen to provide funds for Moody so that he could devote full time to the ministry.

Horatio's life was about to be challenged in ways he never imagined. The first test would be by fire. He had traveled across the state line into Indiana to evaluate a piece of real estate he wished to purchase. After sunset little Annie drew her mother's attention to a peculiar glow that was visible on the southern horizon. Thinking it was only the lights of Chicago, Anna dismissed the child's inquisitiveness and began preparations for bedtime. Annie was adamant that the illumination was much more than that. As she gazed at the sky, Anna caught a glimpse of columns of flame shooting heavenward and clouds of black smoke hovering over the city. The words formed in her horrified mind: Chicago is on fire! Assuring the children that they were in no danger because of the distance from the city, she gathered her girls close as they prayed for God's protection and for the poor souls affected by the fire. Of one thing she was certain: Horatio would make his way home to them by any means if at all possible.

Meanwhile in Indiana, Horatio had picked up a local newspaper that bore the headline, "Chicago in Ashes!"

Tossing his toast and the newspaper aside, he ran for the station to book a seat on the earliest possible train. He dashed to the tracks and jumped aboard, praying for his beloved family all the while. The train struggled through to the south side of Chicago, and when he disembarked, he was horrified to see the state of the city. Flames leapt from building to building; every possible conveyance had been loaded with personal goods in attempts to save as much as possible. The streets were littered with people who, in the rush to escape, had been badly injured or, in some cases, trampled to death by the terrified mob.

Helping to direct as many as he could to safety, Horatio finally reached the north shore of the city. He was appalled as looters ran past carrying armloads of plunder taken from abandoned homes and businesses. Author Rachel Phillips wrote of that time:

> But in the midst of his own despair, Horatio also saw heroes entering burning buildings in efforts to save strangers . . . . men and women threw their arms around the weeping and distraught, sharing food, water, blankets, and wagons . . . .

When night came, the city did not darken, still illuminated with the ghastly, unnatural glare of the fire. Neither did the winds subside. Horatio coughed as clouds of acrid, choking smoke tried to smother him. He had hoped to outrun the fire. He realized, with horror, the fire had outdistanced him with ease and was racing northward . . . . toward Lake View. An evil dragon that engorged itself on everything living and dead in its path, the fire grew every moment . . . . He followed the train track north . . . . The names of [his family] became a refrain that kept him moving, a rhythm that pushed his legs far beyond their usual strength.[7]

Horatio reached home to find his wife and daughters safe. He reeked of smoke and perspiration, but neither he, Anna, nor the children minded. He was home—to a house filled with refugee friends from Chicago—and his loving family.

2

O nce the fire had been extinguished, Horatio tried to put his business life back together. The towering flames had destroyed his beautiful office and reduced his law library collected over the years to ashes. The business district that had surrounded his office building lay in rubble. Offices, banking establishments, hotels, and churches—gone! After digging through the wreckage for hours, Horatio came to the realization that only his fire-proof safe had withstood the heat. He, like so many other businessmen in Chicago, would be forced to rebuild. The funds he had invested in property would provide little return in the short-term; every available dollar would be plowed into rebuilding—not in expansion.

As with so many of his friends, Horatio had shifted into survival mode. Despite the deprivation surrounding them, the Spaffords managed to keep the family home in Lake View, although one guest made it all but unlivable. A woman known only as Aunty Sims had, as a result of the conflagration, been deposited on their doorstep by a wagon driver. Her husband had abandoned her years before the first spark erupted into flames in Chicago. Although querulous and a daily source of irritation and exasperation, the children enjoyed her stories and she, in turn, became devoted to the Spafford family. Sadly, the harangues she leveled at the family for one reason or another finally drove Anna beyond her limitations—to the point the family physician suggested to Horatio that he take his wife away for a protracted trip.

Horatio quickly determined that a two-year sabbatical in Europe would be the very thing to restore Anna to full health and began planning their itinerary. He had also learned that his friend Dwight L. Moody would be holding a series of evangelistic crusades in England. It would be the perfect time for a trip. According to Corts:

> So, in late summer 1873, reservations were made to go first to France, then to Switzerland, over a period of about two years. He made plans

for Maggie and Annie, the two oldest girls to attend a Swiss boarding school. [The governess] Mademoiselle Nicolette would accompany . . . . the two younger girls, Bessie and Tanetta, and they would lodge nearby. Horatio and Anna would be free to travel for several months in Europe as a second honeymoon . . . . It was a grand plan, not uncommon among the well-to-do.[8]

Horatio booked passage for himself and his family, but at the last moment was forced to cancel his own reservation due to having received an offer on a piece of property along Lake Michigan. He insisted that his wife, children, and the nanny continue on to Europe where he would join them as soon as possible. A close friend and neighbor, Mrs. Daniel Goodwin, Jr. and her three children, Goertner, Lulu and Julia, decided to join the Spaffords at the last minute. On November 15, 1873, Anna, their four daughters, Annie, Maggie, Bessie, and Tanetta—ages eleven, nine, seven, and two—nanny, Nicolet, and the Goodwin family boarded the *SS Ville du Havre* in New York City and set sail for Great Britain.

In the wee hours of the morning on November 22, about 1,500 miles from their port of departure, tragedy struck.

The ship carrying the Spafford family collided with the Scottish three-masted iron clipper, the *Loch Earn*. Jolted awake by the impact and the resulting alarm, Anna and Nicolet struggled to get the children from their staterooms to the deck of the ship. The lifeboats were unusable, for they had been painted and had dried stuck fast to the railing of the ship. As panic seized those onboard, Maggie stepped beside her mother and said, "Mama, God will take care of us." Annie added, "The sea is His and He made it."[9]

As the passengers amassed under the night sky, the captain tried to convince them that all would be well. In actuality, the iron clipper had almost split the *Ville du Harve* in half. The travelers soon realized that they were in a very grave situation and frantically began to try to pry the lifeboats from the deck. Their efforts were only partially successful, and pandemonium ensued as passengers vied for the few spaces available on the freed crafts. The captain of the *Loch Earn* had no concept of the damage sustained by the *Ville du Harve*. Shortly after the collision, he saw a lifeboat containing four crewmen who were rowing toward his ship. He called to them asking if their ship was badly damaged. The Frenchmen aboard the boat did not understand the question, nor did the captain comprehend their reply.

Help that could have been forthcoming was delayed by the lack of communication, something the *Loch Earn* captain would not know for some time.

All too soon, two of the masts on the sailing ship collapsed onto the deck smashing everything beneath them, including several of the desperate travelers. Only twelve minutes elapsed from impact until the *Ville du Harve* broke into two sections and sank below the murky waters of the Atlantic Ocean. The captain of the *Loch Earn* worked valiantly to save as many of the party from the doomed ship as possible, but was only able to rescue sixty-one passengers and twenty-six crew members; 226 passengers and crew died.

Anna was one of the survivors, and was found bruised and unconscious atop a board floating in the Atlantic. Nicolet and the Spaffords' four daughters were among those swept to a watery grave, their bodies never recovered. Bertha Spafford Vester, a daughter later born to the couple, wrote that she found a scrap of paper on which her mother had written:

> "I had no vision during the struggle in the water at the time of the shipwreck, only the conviction that any earnest soul, brought face to face with its maker, must have; I realized

that my Christianity must be real. There was no room here for self-pity, or for the practice of that Christianity that always favours and condones itself and its own, rendering innocuous the sharp two-edged sword of the Word which was intended to separate soul from spirit and the desires and thoughts and intents of the heart. This soft religion was as far removed from Christ's practice of Christianity as east from west. Nothing but a robust Christianity could save me then and now". . . . Mother told me, long after, that when she came back to consciousness in the boat and knew she had been recalled to life, that her first realization was complete despair. How could she face life without her children? Horrible as was her physical suffering, her mental anguish was worse. Her life had been bound up in her little girls. What was life worth now, and what could it ever be without them?[10]

Anna later told Bertha that "when she came back to consciousness in the boat, and she knew she had been recalled to life, her first realization was complete despair . . . .

Then, it was as if a voice spoke to her: 'You are spared for a purpose. You have work to do.'"[11]

The passengers who had been rescued by the badly damaged *Loch Earn* were cared for as well as possible by the crew aboard the vessel. The women were provided with whatever clothing the crew should scavenge together. As the vastness of the sea and the horror of the devastation swept over the survivors, a ship appeared on the horizon. The *Trimountain* was a cargo vessel with a full rigging of sails to propel it across the ocean. Spotting the schooner at rest in the waves, Captain William W. Urquhart sent a message to Captain Robertson offering hospitality and the willingness to take the entire contingent of the *Loch Earn* aboard. The survivors made ready for a mid-ocean transfer from one ship to another—a risky venture.

Refusing to abandon his ship for the safety of the American cargo vessel, Captain Robertson was determined to see his vessel safely to shore. Of the three *Ville du Harve* passengers left aboard the *Loch Earn* two were clerics— Rev. Nathaniel Weiss and Rev. Emile Cook—the third was Leopold Zaffiere, a badly injured fireman from the sunken ship. Rev. Weiss was as gravely hurt as the fireman; Cook recognized his friend's inability to withstand the move and determined to stay with him as long as necessary. With heavy hearts, the crew and remaining survivors watched as the *Trimountain* set sail.

The captain of the *Loch Earn* then ordered his crewmen to make the ship as seaworthy as possible. Looking much like a lone leaf hurtling downhill, propelled by a rushing mountain stream, the schooner floundered from trough to trough in the rough waters. Unable to steer a course and taking on water, the vessel was at the mercy of the waves. But what better traveling companions to have than two men who trusted in the One "Who has measured the waters in the hollow of His hand." (Isaiah 40:12, NKJV) While Rev. Weiss was badly injured, some thought even to the point of death, Rev. Cook began to hold brief services daily. As the Word was shared, Weiss began to recover.

On December 11, Rev. Dr. Andrew Thompson shared a missive with the crowd gathered in Edinburgh, Scotland to hear Dwight L. Moody. It had been written by the mother of one of the passengers aboard the *Loch Earn*. She wrote of Rev. Cook's last service aboard the ship:

> Mr. Cook told them of his own hope, that death to him would be eternal life, and he urgently entreated them to put their trust in 'Him who was mighty to save.' At the same time

he told them he had no doubt they would be rescued, that even then a vessel was speeding to save them, that God had answered their prayers, that next day as morning dawned they would see her . . . .

As morning dawned every eye was strained to see the promised ship. There truly she was, and the *British Queen* bore down upon them . . . . One thing is remarkable—the officer in charge on board the *British Queen* had a most unaccountable feeling that there was something for him to do, and three times during the night he changed the course of the vessel, bearing northward. He told the watch to keep a sharp lookout for a ship, and immediately on sighting the *Loch Earn* bore down upon her. At first he thought she had been abandoned, as she lay helpless in the trough of the sea, but soon they saw her signal of distress. It seems to me a remarkable instance of faith on the one side and a guiding Providence on the other. After they were taken on board the pilot-boat that brought them into Plymouth, at noon, when they for the last time joined together in prayer, Mr. Cook read to them the account of Paul's shipwreck [Acts 27-28], showing the similarity of their experience.[12]

When the *Trimountain* delivered her cargo of bruised, battered, and distraught refugees to Cardiff, Wales, Anna sent a cable that devastated Horatio Spafford, who had been awaiting word of their safe arrival in the French port. It said simply:

> Saved alone what shall I do. Mrs. Goodwin children Willie Culver lost go with Lorriaux until answer reply Porclain 64 Rue Aboukir Paris. —Spafford[13]

With the lack of communication during that particular time, Horatio had not been particularly disturbed when he had not heard from Anna. He assumed that he would soon receive notification of their arrival at Ville du Harve, France. Almost a week after the ship carrying his beloved family was lost Horatio received the shocking and overwhelming cable from Anna, sent not from Ville du Harve, but from Cardiff, Wales. Stunned and sick with grief, he reeled from room to room in the house and tried with battered mind to plan his immediate departure to join Anna. He sent for his close friend Evangelist Daniel W. Whittle who had the sad assignment of consoling the inconsolable Horatio. In an equally concise cable to Anna, her husband promised to join her as quickly as he could. Though separated by miles of ocean, the Spaffords were bound by the scarlet cord of God's unrelenting love and grace. Like Job, Horatio had been beset by unimaginable troubles; unlike Job's wife, Anna stood firm in her faith and with the echo of her little Annie's last words: "Mama, God will take care of us."

Horatio and Daniel Goodwin, whose family had also been lost in the shipwreck, traveled to New York City where they boarded the Cunard Lines ship, *Abyssinia*. While at sea, the captain of the liner worked to pinpoint the probable location of the wreck that had sent the families of the two men to a watery grave. About midway in their voyage, the captain summoned Spafford and Goodwin to his cabin and revealed that they were crossing the fateful spot. Slipping from the captain's stateroom, Horatio returned to his cabin where he sat with pen in hand and wrote what was to become one of Christendom's most beloved hymns, "It Is Well With My Soul":

> When peace, like a river, attendeth my way,
> When sorrows like sea billows roll;
> Whatever my lot, Thou has taught me to say,

It is well, it is well, with my soul.

Though Satan should buffet,

though trials should come,

Let this blest assurance control,

That Christ has regarded my helpless estate,

And hath shed His own blood for my soul.

My sin, oh, the bliss of this glorious thought!

My sin, not in part but the whole,

Is nailed to the cross, and I bear it no more,

Praise the Lord, praise the Lord, O my soul!

(*Refrain*) It is well, with my soul,

It is well, it is well, with my soul.[14]

Writer James Watkins tells the rest of the story surrounding the writing of this beautiful hymn:

> The tune was written by Philip P. Bliss . . . .
> The hymn was first sung by Bliss himself before
> a large gathering of ministers hosted by Moody
> on November 24, 1876. Just one month later, on
> December 29, 1876, Bliss and wife were trav-
> eling to Chicago by train. As the train passed
> over a trestle near Ashtabula, Ohio, the bridge
> collapsed and the passenger coaches plunged 75
> feet into the icy river. Philip was able to escape

through a window, but his wife was pinned in the wreckage. As he went back to free his wife, a fire broke out through the wooden cars and both were burned beyond recognition.

[A number of] tragic deaths surround the hymn, and yet those affected by them, could say, "It is well with my soul."[15]

The Spaffords were reunited in Paris where Anna had been taken to recuperate. Nothing was recorded by either Horatio or Anna about that heartrending and emotional reunion. Some things are too sacred for words. On the way home to Chicago, the two traveled first to London, where they were met by D. L. Moody and Ira Sanky. The men were overwhelmed with grief for what their friends had suffered and lost.

In November 1876, Anna would give birth to a son, Horatio Goertner (named for their neighbor's son who had drowned with the Spafford daughters); in 1878, to daughter Bertha; and in 1881 to daughter Grace. No strangers to tragedy, the Spaffords suffered another grievous loss: Their son, Horatio, fell victim to a deadly case of scarlet fever and succumbed during the winter of 1880.

3

Back home in Lake View, the Spaffords were targeted with taunts of faithlessness, improper parenting, heartlessness, and other unkind labels following the deaths of their five children. The pious practitioners of imprudence thought Anna unfeeling because she had not attended her son's funeral—she was still quarantined along with young Bertha. Horatio, who conducted his offspring's funeral, was labeled callous because of his choice. The words and charges pierced the hearts of the two grieving parents and ultimately drove them from Lake View to the shores of the Mediterranean, and inland to the city of Jerusalem. Anna was persuaded that they would find a much longed-for peace in the land where Jesus had lived and walked. He was, after all, "a man of sorrows, and acquainted with grief." (Isaiah 53:3, KJV) Horatio wrote to a close friend, "Jerusalem is where my Lord lived, suffered and conquered, and I too wish to learn how to live, suffer and, especially, to conquer."[16]

Leaving behind anything of value in Chicago, they packed only a single trunk including a few letters and papers of sentimental value. The Spaffords and a small contingent of men, women, and children, dubbed the "Overcomers," emigrated to what would later become the nation of Israel. Upon arrival in London, a British newspaper published the following paragraph dated September 8, 1881:

> H.C. Spafford, of Lake View, leader of the new sect of "Overcomers," arrived in London with a band of these peculiar believers, including several children, en route to Palestine. They will proceed to the Mount of Olives, where they expect to receive a new and direct revelation from the Lord.[17]

In Jaffa, one of the oldest port cities in Israel, the group would have been met by the sights described earlier by members of the Palestine Exploration Foundation: Charles Wilson, Claude R. Conder, and Horatio Kitchener. In Volume Two of their extensive notes on the land, the men recorded:

The town rises in terraces from the water; it is surrounded on all sides by the wall and ditch, which are decaying rapidly. The port is very bad; the ordinary entrance is through a narrow reef, but in stormy weather the boats go out by a passage on the north side.

The bazaars are among the best in Palestine. The principal buildings in the town are the Latin Hospice, the Serai in the centre of the town, the mosque towards the north. The quarantine is outside the walls on the south, and the Greek monastery on the east, on which side a new gate was made in 1869. The wall is here pulled down...

There is a lighthouse near the custom-house of the town, and near this a little mosque, said to mark the site of the Crusading Church of St. Peter. The principal bazaar is in the north-east corner of the town, just outside the original land gate. The walls date from the end of the eighteenth century, at which period the town was re-built, having been almost entirely destroyed in the fifteenth century. They were commenced by the English, and continued by the Turks after the storming by Kleber in 1799 . . . . Most of the area to the east of the city was agriculture - mainly growing oranges which were exported from the port. On the south and north are vast areas of sand.[18]

Moving into a house in the Old City of Jerusalem, the Overcomers established an early commune—the American Colony. Spafford and his friends were determined not to proselytize the Jews, but rather to simply serve them by meeting the needs of the underprivileged, distressed, and exiled. Simon Sebag Montefiore wrote of the Spaffords and their settlement in Jerusalem:

> In 1881, the Overcomers—thirteen adults and three children, who became the nucleus of the American Colony—settled in a large house just inside the Damascus Gate . . . . the sect thrived as they preached the Second Coming . . . . and developed their colony into a philanthropic, evangelical beehive of hospitals, orphanages, soup-kitchens, a shop, their own photography studio and a school. Their success attracted the hostility of the long-serving American consul-ate-clergyman, Selah Merrill, an anti-Semitic

Massachusetts Congregationalist clergyman, Andover professor and inept archaeologist. For twenty years Merrill tried to destroy the Colonists, accusing them of charlatanism, anti-Americanism, lewdness and child-kidnapping. He threatened to send his guards to horsewhip them.[19]

The first year in the foreign land was a difficult one for the American pilgrims—new foods, languages, traditions, and modes of dress. Jerusalem was truly a multicultural city. Their first Christmas there was bleak, especially for the Spaffords who remembered past cheerful holidays surrounded by their daughters and son. Because people tend to think of that region as hot, dry, and dusty, Horatio and Anna may have been unprepared for the cold winds that can blow in the Middle East in December. Three years later, the scene was much different, for the inhabitants of the American Colony had surrounded themselves with friends—Europeans, Jews, and Arabs alike.

While the men of the Colony became teachers of English to wealthy Jews and Arabs, the women set about to minister to the women in the city. They simply met for a time of prayer, Bible study, sewing, and singing. It was music that proved to be the draw as people gathered to sing hymns. Even when English was a challenge, they managed to hum along, or simply enjoyed the classically-trained voice of Anna Spafford.

As months turned into years, the members of the American Colony found themselves ministering to the physical and mental needs of the men, women, and children who showed up at their always-open door. Corts wrote of their commitment:

> The members of the American Colony did not shrink from the unusual number of mentally ill people attracted to Jerusalem .... And these they fed and sheltered unless they posed a direct threat to the other residents of the household .... Because the Colony supplied food, shelter, and clothing, as well as medicine and nursing, to many indigent people, enormous costs mounted steadily. At one time, more than 150 people, many of them helpless or ill, resided at the American Colony .... Caring friends and relatives often sent monetary gifts to help meet expenses, but the American Colony fell deeper and deeper into debt .... Fortunately, Horatio

maintained excellent relations with their Jerusalem neighbors, whose financial help kept the charitable services running.[20]

The poverty that threatened could not quench the love that God had placed in the hearts of Horatio and Anna Spafford for the people of Jerusalem. They came to love the hills and valleys, the farms and orchards, the Jews and the Arabs in the land their Lord had trod.

The colony became noted for its hospitality and service to others. It was a frequent stopping place for dignitaries. John H. Finley, appointed to head the American Red Cross in Jerusalem following the First World War and a dedicated Christian, visited often. The German vice-consul and his family were also regular visitors in the home of Horatio and Anna. The Spaffords greeted them warmly as welcome guests—except for their young son. When the family arrived at the gate, Anna would designate someone to watch over the out-of-control child. The little terror was Rudolf Hess, who would become Adolf Hitler's private secretary and the third highest person in the deadly Nazi regime. Another noted visitor to The Colony was General Charles "Chinese" Gordon. During his survey of Jerusalem, Claude Conder became convinced that the actual Mount Calvary—the

Hill of the Skull—was located on a rocky mount outside the northern side of the city. It was near a place known as Jeremiah's Grotto. The hill looks amazingly like a human skull. It was, however, British General Gordon, a distinguished soldier and war hero during the Boxer Rebellion in China, who lent his name to the site that is still today often called "Gordon's Calvary." Gordon spent hours on the flat rooftop of the Spafford home reading and meditating on the Bible. One day during his meditations, he called out:

> Look, the rocky ridge looks like a huge skull.
> This is the true Golgotha! Not the Golgotha in
> the Church of the Holy Sepulchre![21]

It is said the general was so passionate about his discovery that he pitched a tent on top of the hill. Inaccurately, it is Gordon, and not Conder, who is credited with the discovery.

In 1888, William Blackstone of whom we will learn more later and his daughter, Flora, visited Palestine and toured the area on horseback. They spent time at the American Colony with Horatio and Anna. The two men had met in Chicago when both were active in the ministry of D. L. Moody. The trip abroad took about a year, and concluded in London. When Blackstone returned to his home in Oak Park, Illinois, he was interviewed by a reporter who was curious about the group that had left Chicago eight years before to establish a colony in Jerusalem. Blackstone reported that the Americans spent their time in "works of charity and devotion . . . . constantly engaged in feeding the hungry and nursing the sick. Their house is a sort of a free hotel for everyone who needs shelter. Bedouins, Arabs, Jews, and all sorts of people drop in there and are kindly entertained."[22]

Reverend George J. Adams was another of the Americans who helped to found the American Colony in Jaffa. He and his followers from the Church of the Messiah in Jonesport, Maine, were persuaded that God was leading them as He had led Abraham to the Promised Land. They felt it their duty to lay the groundwork for those who would follow to the Holy Land. Many of those brave pioneers, including Horatio, who died of malaria on October 16, 1888, and Anna Spafford, would not live to see the rebirth of Israel.

In 1896, Anna and the original group of Overcomers were joined by a group of Swedish farmers. The influx of new people caused an overflow in their small space. The mansion of Rabbah Husseini was leased to provide more room for the sect. In 1902, the grandfather of the late British actor Peter Ustinov—Baron Plato von Ustinov—petitioned for permission to send guests from his hotel in Jaffa to stay at the American Colony. It was the beginning of its conversion into a guest house.

A July 4, 1920 article from the *Minneapolis Sunday Tribune* recounted the past and the perseverance of the American Colony. The journalist described the Colony as a "noble band of American men and women [who] have been holding for nearly 40 years a lonely outpost of American civilization in a strange far-off land, overcoming persecutions, poverty, and the hardship of the World War by following the Golden Rule in living a life of Christian charity."[23]

The Spafford Children's Center was founded in 1925 by their daughter, Bertha Spafford Vester. It is a memorial to her mother Anna who died in April 1923. Spafford Children's Center still stands in the Old City of Jerusalem where its employees care for more than 30,000 children annually. It meets the physical, mental, and spiritual needs of underprivileged youngsters. Counselors are provided for the children and/or their families; summer outings and camps are a regular part of the curriculum. The Spafford dream of lending a helping hand to those in need lives on in Jerusalem.

LAURENCE OLIPHANT

As long as in the heart, within,
A Jewish soul still yearns,
And onward, towards the ends of the east,
An eye still looks toward Zion.
Our hope is not yet lost,
The ancient hope,
To return to the land of our fathers,
The city where David encamped.

—Text of Tikvateinu by
NAFTALI HERZ IMBER[24]

1

L aurence Lowry Oliphant was known alternatively as a voyager, diplomat, a British Member of Parliament, a prophet, author of a satirical novel, *Piccadilly*, and of several travel-related books. The only descendant of Sir Anthony Oliphant and wife, Maria Catherine Campbell, Laurence was born in Cape Colony, a British outpost in South Africa in 1829. When he was eight or nine, he and his mother returned to Scotland, and while there, Sir Anthony was posted to Colombo, Ceylon—today Sri Lanka—as Chief Justice. As an offspring of landowners who could live solely on estate rental income, Anthony and his six siblings shared the lineage required to open doors for successful careers. Two of his brothers made their marks in the East India Company and another, Thomas, became a noted artist and composer. His brother, James, married three times and presented Anthony's son, young Laurence, with an astonishing number of first cousins—eighteen.

According to author Bart Casey, the Oliphants were quite religious:

> Externally, Anthony and Maria played their parts as leaders in government and society, but at home they were also soul mates—both conservative "evangelical" believers in the gospels of Jesus Christ and the certainty of his Second Coming and judgment. In addition, Anthony was a follower of the Scottish divine, Edward Irving, who not only preached an imminent Second Coming, but also emphasized the importance of returning the Jews to Palestine . . . . they saw the development of Laurence as a devout Christian as one of their most serious responsibilities. . . .

> Thus, from the start, Laurence had these multiple priorities set for him: to uphold a strict and moral code of behavior; to become a positive force for improving other people's lives on earth; and to succeed at a career serving Queen and country in the British Empire.[25]

Health issues had forced Maria to return to Scotland for treatment in the late 1830s. As she received health care, mother and son divided their time between Anthony's ancestral home in Condie, Scotland, and his brother James' home in Wimbledon on the outskirts of London. Maria was finally well enough to join Anthony in Sri Lanka early in 1841; Laurence remained in Scotland to complete the school term.

Laurence and his tutor traveled to Sri Lanka in the winter of 1841 to rejoin Sir Anthony and Maria. The trip today would take approximately ten hours, but took the duo sixty days by various watercraft and a caravan that took them across the desert from Cairo, Egypt to Suez. There, they boarded another ship for their last leg home. The elder Oliphant settled his little family at an estate named "Alcove" in an area known as Captain's Gardens. Father and son have been given credit for importing tea from China to their estate in Nuwara Eliya, Ceylon. It has today become a major tea-growing area in Sri Lanka.

At the age of seventeen, Laurence found himself back in England and settled with a tutor to prepare for his studies at Cambridge. Just as he was about to take the plunge into academic life, Sir Anthony and Maria arrived with the announcement that they were to spend the next twenty-four months enjoying a grand tour of the Continent. Laurence began immediately to make his case for taking the journey with them; he won, and off they went. In his own words: "I found myself, to my great delight, transferred from the quiet of a Warwickshire vicarage to the Champs Élysées in Paris."[26]

In 1850, the Oliphants returned home to Ceylon. It was decided that Laurence would not travel to England to further his education; instead, he settled into his father's office as an apprentice attorney. At that time and in that place, it was permissible to be "called to the bar" without actually having taken an exam. From his father's office, Laurence would learn how a man of integrity operated, as well as gain experience from his father's knowledge and example.

Following a commotion in the office of the British governor in Colombo, Sir Anthony returned to London to aid in the inquiry against the governor, Lord Torrington. When the matter was resolved, he made his way back home in the company of Nepalese ambassador, Prince Jung Bahadur. Sir Anthony and the young royal left the ship at Colombo. The Oliphant family joined him for dinner where Laurence was petitioned to accompany the prince on a journey from Colombo back to his home in Kathmandu. Along the route, the group halted for elephant hunting—an attempt to capture wild elephants to be trained for use by the Nepalese army. Laurence wrote of the wild rush in his first manuscript, *A Journey to Katmandu* (sic):

> Away we went . . . . and I looked upon it as a miracle that every bone in my body was not broken. Sometimes I was jerked into a sitting posture, and, not being able to get my heels from under me in time, they received a violent blow. A moment later I was thrown forward on my face, only righting myself in time to see a huge impending branch, which I had to escape by slipping rapidly down the crupper [a loop of leather attached to a saddle], taking all the skin off my toes in so doing, and what would have been more serious, the branch nearly taking my head off if I did not stoop low enough.[27]

After his return to Ceylon, he found that great change had come to the Oliphant household—his father had decided to retire and return to England. In October 1851, Sir Anthony and Lady Maria found themselves in London where Laurence determined to study for admission to the bar there and in Edinburgh. While studying, he kept an eye open for his next travel adventure; one was not long in coming. His good friend, Oswald Smith, invited Laurence to join him for a hunting and fishing trip to Russia. Their target: salmon and white bear. Fortunately for the hapless animals, Russian customs agents levied an exorbitant tax on their equipment. It was swiftly returned to England while the intrepid explorers continued on their way across the interior by boat and wagon.

The description of their trek was published in 1853 as: *The Russian Shores of the Black Sea in the Autumn of 1852 with a Voyage Down the Volga and a Tour Through the Country of the Don Cossacks*--not a title that flows trippingly off the tongue. It was, however, a major success and won its author and friend, Oswald, a visit to army headquarters at Horse Guards Parade in Whitehall. There, the two travelers were quizzed about the sights and fortifications they had seen along the way. Why? In October 1853 the Crimean War broke out between Russia and an alliance of nations consisting of France, the British Empire, the Ottoman Empire, and Sardinia. Writer Bart Casey noted:

> The travelers gave the senior British gen-
> erals, Lord de Ros and Sir John Burgoyne, a
> complete description of the fortifications of
> the Sebastopol harbor—and asserted the lack

of any fortifications on the southern approach to the town of Balaclava.... He [Laurence] even suggested a strategy for a successful attack to Sir John, although he knew he was out of his element.... Now all of Laurence's energies and aspirations were focused on taking part in some way, in his country's actions in the Crimean campaign.[28]

Laurence's opportunity to serve came not through the war office or from a newspaper seeking a correspondent, but through the office of a friend of the Oliphants—James Bruce, Eighth Earl of Elgin. The career diplomat had been posted to Canada as Governor General and offered Laurence the post of personal secretary for a very specific mission: negotiating a trade agreement between the United States and Canada. Laurence accepted the proposal and soon found himself on his way via train to Washington D.C. He wrote in his journal of the perplexing jargon that surrounded him there:

I am getting perfectly stunned with harangues upon political questions I don't understand with the nomenclature appropriate to each. Besides Whigs and Democrats, there are Hard Shells, Soft Shells, and Free Soilers, and Disunionists, and Federals, to say nothing of filibusters, pollywogs and a host of other nicknames.[29]

Once business was concluded in Washington, the British legation turned again toward Canada and Spencer Wood, Lord Elgin's estate near Quebec. Laurence was thwarted from returning to England and his hopes of Crimean action by an appointment as Superintendent-General of Indian Affairs. He was not ready to give up his freedom of travel, but the office did afford him the opportunity to visit the Canadian West at the expense of Queen Victoria. Laurence could have coasted through his assignment, but spent his time engaged in settling tribal clashes, visiting schools, and obtaining from the Indians half a million acres of land on an island in Lake Huron. And, although he was separated from his father and mother by a vast ocean, he remained a faithful correspondent. Having been raised in an evangelical home, one surprising letter expressed Laurence's exasperation with being so far removed from God:

> Everything around me testifies to the existence of a Being who is all pervading; but the Son is nowhere visible and does not, so to speak, force Himself upon the senses. It is a totally

different act of the mind which is required to accept Him as a positive fact. [30]

Laurence seemed to be searching for a faith that was honest and tangible, one not reliant on what he had learned at his mother's knee, but which was based on his personal experience with God. Unfortunately, his search took him into some rather "otherworldly" avenues including, for instance, the still-active Swedenborg Society that believes "God has many names, depending on the beliefs/religion of the individual; the Holy Spirit is not God; the Trinity does not exist; Jesus Christ's death did not atone for our sin; salvation comes by practicing what you believe, whatever religion it might be; the afterlife is spiritual, but dependent on how well you lived in your physical body."[31] He also at varying times followed the Second Great Awakening, self-realization, transcendentalism, and Spiritism.

Laurence searched for spiritual truth albeit in some very unlikely places, but in the meantime, his mentor Lord Elgin had received a new posting—China. Almost immediately, he requested that Laurence return to his former post of personal secretary. He served Lord Elgin for two long years, and then set sail for England and a reunion with his parents. During the voyage, he dreamed that he talked with his father who informed Laurence he had died. He recounted the vision to his friends aboard ship and was chided for his somber reaction. When the vessel docked at the next port-of-call and mail was collected, Laurence learned that his father had, indeed, dropped dead suddenly on the very same evening that the dream unfolded. The devastating loss caused both Laurence and his mother to resort to the company of the many mediums and spiritualists that inhabited London. Pitiful and counterfeit attempts were made to reach Sir Anthony in the afterlife. As a last resort, the mother and son contacted American medium and Universalist Thomas Lake Harris. It would be a fateful meeting with long-lasting effects for the Oliphant family.

2

I t was Oliphant's continued search for spiritual fulfillment that had led him to Thomas Lake Harris, a disciple of Swedish mystic practitioner Emmanuel Swedenborg.
Harris had established the Mountain Grove Community of
Spiritualists commune in Virginia—a transitory undertaking
that lasted only a couple of years. After the collapse of his
communal experiment, Harris returned to England where
for several years he led a congregation in London. When that
endeavor also ended in failure, Harris moved on to Dutchess
County, New York where he settled in Armenia, moving later
to Brocton, New York. There, among other endeavors, he
established a commune and began a wine-making venture.

It was, perhaps, Laurence's introduction to politics
that finally drove him to join Harris' group in New York.

After leaving the employ of Lord Elgin, Laurence began a career in Parliament where he discovered the unsettling methods used by various statesmen to advance their own careers and agendas. He entered the fray as a zealous backer of Prime Minister William Gladstone's measures to pass reform bills in support of improving the conditions for lower class workers. Those efforts were defeated, only to be revived with minor changes under the auspices of Benjamin Disraeli, Gladstone's replacement. Biographer Bart Casey wrote of those "worst of times" in *The Double Life of Laurence Oliphant*:

> It was in the middle of this legislative wrangling that Laurence's distant cousin and prolific author, Margaret Oliphant, met him one evening in 1867 in a visitors' gallery at the House of Commons. It was late in the day and they were both awaiting the speeches for Disraeli's re-introduction of the reform bill, and although they had met before, Margaret said this occasion led them to the closest conversation they had ever had. Several things from that evening deeply surprised her: first, the degree of utter contempt Laurence had for the politicians;

and second, his de-bunking of the spiritualist mediums . . . . as quacks. She was also just as surprised by his assertions that exciting new paths to spiritual enlightenment were actually manifesting themselves to those open enough to receive them . . . . Above all, she was startled at how bitter he was . . . . In the spring of 1867, [Thomas Lake] Harris could sense his new disciple was at the breaking point, and, no doubt with the urging of Lady Oliphant, gave permission for Laurence to join his industrious community in Amenia . . . .[32]

Laurence found life under Harris' thumb to be a constant round of hard labor—mucking stables and cleaning and polishing boots. Later, he would graduate to living in a two-room hovel in a shed. To furnish his dwelling, Laurence was required to make furniture out of whatever materials could be found and working from early morning until late at night. The entire compound was charged with the task of caring for Harris' needs.

As Laurence became more acclimated to life among the cult members, newspapers began to spread rumors about Harris and his followers. There were stories that the children were sadly neglected and forced to work in the gardens or at household duties instead of attending school. Some members began to question Harris' iron-fisted hold over the occupants and left the commune. In 1870, Laurence also left the community, or rather was sent out by Harris to earn money that was to be deposited into the general fund. After several aborted attempts to gain a post, Laurence was saved by the Franco-Prussian War. *The Times* offered him an assignment covering the action. Oliphant found himself back in the midst of a war, and typically keen to enter the fight.

Laurence continued his wild rush through life. He had done everything from dangling over a precipice while climbing Ceylon's holy mountain, Adam's Peak, to his elephant hunting adventure in Nepal, traveling across Russia in a cart, and even once having his hair parted by an errant bullet in France during the Franco-Prussian War. It was the latter that drove Laurence back to Harris' compound and to his mother whom he had not been allowed to see before his departure for Europe. Upon his arrival, he discovered that her health had suffered during his absence. Laurence, however, was soon ordered to return to France, and given permission by Harris to take Lady Oliphant with him. Upon arrival in Paris, the duo rented a house near the city's center.

Laurence continued to work as a correspondent for *The Times*, a job that provided a rather substantial salary and a sizeable expense account.

It was in Paris that he would meet his future wife, Alice le Strange and her mother, Lady Wynne-Finch. Alice was recruited as a member of Harris' cult, and with the leader's blessing, she and Laurence married in June 1872. One of the quirks of the cult was that cohabitation was forbidden for all except Harris and a few chosen, mostly female, members. The marriage of Laurence and Alice remained unconsummated for twelve years, and for much of that time, the heavy-handed Harris even forbade correspondence between the two. Their short separation turned into years with neither knowing just how long they would be apart. Perhaps there were times that Laurence must have wondered why he and Alice even married and whether or not they would ever have a life together. This was especially true since there was some speculation that Alice may have shared Harris' bed as part of the man's twisted theology.

In 1878, Laurence returned to England alone; there he continued his career as a war correspondent wherever political clashes ended up on the battlefield. During his sojourn, the Russians and Ottoman Turks began a series of power plays that would cause great unrest in the region, later culminating in the events that would launch World War I.

The Ottoman Empire was undermined as a result of the war with Russia and its march toward Constantinople. Laurence began to study various scenarios that would aid the Turks in retaining hold on some of the provinces under their dominion, such as Palestine. The war had wreaked severe havoc on the Empire's bankroll, leaving its leaders with serious deficits. Added to that issue was the expanse of undeveloped lands just waiting for the Russians to dash in and claim the area for Tsar Alexander III. Laurence developed a plan that, while not addressing all the complications faced by the Turks, might provide some relief for its embattled ruler.

In 1878, twelve years before Theodor Herzl initiated the Zionist movement, Laurence Oliphant began his quest for a Jewish national homeland in Palestine. As a British resident, Oliphant had connections both to diplomats and Christian Evangelicals. For those who disparaged Zionism, he was said to have been a classic example of a Christian Zionist—eccentric and unconventional. However, he was also very competent and prudent. His life was a combination of the utmost in public propriety and organizational reliability. The disadvantage was that he was deeply caught up in what was considered to be, then and now, the obsessive religious sect formed by Thomas Lake Harris. It was called the Brotherhood of the New Life, with factions in New York and California. While Laurence's association with Scottish editor John Blackwood of *Blackwood's Edinburgh Magazine* was more heartening, his association with Harris had become extremely distressing.

On December 10, 1878, Oliphant wrote to his friend Blackwood. In his missive he laid out the complex new plan for an "Eastern project." It involved land concessions from the Ottomans for the establishment of a Jewish homeland in Palestine:

> My Eastern project is as follows: To obtain a concession from the Turkish Government in the northern and more fertile half of Palestine, which the recent survey of the Palestine Exploration Fund proves to be capable of immense development. Any amount of money can be raised upon it, owing to the belief which people have that they would be fulfilling prophecy and bringing on the end of the world. I don't know why they are so anxious for this latter event, but it makes the commercial speculation easy,

as it is a combination of the financial and sentimental elements which will, I think, ensure success. And it will be a good political move for the Government, as it will enable them to carry out reforms in Asiatic Turkey, provide money for the Porte, and by uniting the French in it, and possibly the Italians, be a powerful religious move against the Russians, who are trying to obtain a hold of the country by their pilgrims. It would also secure the Government a large religious support in this country, as even the Radicals would waive their political in favour of their religious crotchets. I also anticipate a very good subscription in America. I shall probably start about the end of the year for Egypt, as I want to look into the working of the mixed jurisdiction, and then go to Cyprus, Syria, Palestine, and Constantinople. I suppose I shall find plenty to write about, but I do not want it all talked of, though I find it difficult to keep it quiet. Both Lord Beaconsfield and Lord Salisbury are very favourable to my scheme.[33]

In writing the letter, Oliphant was poised and assured regarding the fiscal, spiritual, and governmental facets of the proposal. It resembles a letter he had written to British Foreign Minister Lord Salisbury in 1878. The next year, Oliphant journeyed to Constantinople in an attempt to secure a lease for the northern half of Palestine. It was his intent to establish a Jewish settlement there. Assuming the mantle of unauthorized diplomat, Oliphant was passionate about the restoration of the Jews to their homeland. His book *The Land of Gilead* proposed "Jewish resettlement, under Turkish sovereignty and British protection, of Palestine east of the Jordan."[34]

From a financial point of view, Oliphant thought it would be an easy undertaking. He was aware that the Palestine Exploration Fund (PEF) had promised 40,000 British pounds sterling to an effort he had labeled the "Gilead Plan." And, after all, England and America were rife with monetary support to be had from those submerged in the prophetic Second Coming of Christ. He was certain that the Christadelphians[35] and others would collect offerings to purchase the property in Galilee to fulfill his vision. The PEF agreed to give credence and funds to Oliphant's work. It was also quickly sanctioned by Zionists both in Britain and in the Holy Land. His proposed project was to be based east of the Jordan River—an area that eventually became the Hashemite Kingdom of Jordan.

Oliphant opined in his 1880 book, *The Land of Gilead* that relief might be reached by forming a Colonisation Company. He studied the parameters regarding just who would be the best candidate for the experiment he proposed. He then wrote in the book's introduction:

> The objection to foreigners who were at the same time Christians seemed insurmountable . . . . Moreover, the rivalries of the various Christian sects . . . . would certainly render all attempts at harmonious colonisation abortive. The idea, therefore, of colonising with European Christians was speedily dismissed. [A similar plan to colonize with Arabs was abandoned due to a lack of sufficient funds to establish a colony. Oliphant had determined that there was only one answer to the question of acceptable colonists: European Jews.] There was, in fact, only one race in Europe who were rich, and who did not, therefore, need to appeal to Christian capitalists for money to carry through the whole undertaking . . . . The more I examined the

project from this point of view, the more desirable on political grounds did it appear . . . . The
Jews themselves have borne repeated testimony
to the fact that, so far as they are concerned,
Christian fanaticism in Eastern Europe is far
more bitter than Moslem; and indeed, the position of Jews in Turkey is relatively favoured.[36]

Oliphant's idea gathered significant backing from
various sources including Princess Helena-Christian, the
daughter of Queen Victoria. She penned a letter to British
Prime Minister Disraeli in which she pressed him to consider Laurence's proposal as one worthy of consideration.
Sponsorship by the princess garnered Oliphant an invitation
to dinner with the Prince of Wales at Sandringham where
he discovered that the other guests at the small party were
the prime minister, the foreign secretary, and the ambassador to Austria. So grateful was he for her support that he
dedicated *The Land of Gilead* to "Princess Christian."

3

While Laurence was delving into the heady stratosphere of foreign policy at the Royal Palace, Alice remained under the thumb of Harris in California. She was unable to accompany her husband on his first fact-finding trip to Palestine as he sought to determine the best location for the new project. The next step in the agenda was for him to persuade the Ottoman Sultan and Jewish leaders in Europe that the whole idea was viable. He was joined in Beirut by his long-time friend, Captain Owen Phibbs, a man well-versed in both the mores and languages of the region. Their "expedition" consisted of two servants, a boy, horses and a mule, a ploy to prevent the appearance of wealth. The men and their guides trooped across miles and miles of desert dotted with broken-down cisterns and collapsed storage rooms hewn into the rocks. Laurence's imagination was sparked by the sites of facilities that could be restored and wells that could be resurrected to support colonists in the land.

Instead of sand, rocks, and scrub brush, Oliphant saw a region that could be heavily cultivated. He wrote:

> The valley of the Jordan would act as an enormous hothouse for the new colony. Here might be cultivated palms, cotton, indigo, sugar, rice, sorghum, besides bananas, pineapples, yams, sweet potatoes, and other field and garden produce. Rising a little higher, the country is adapted to tobacco, maize, castor-oil, millet, flax, sesamum [sesame], melons, gourds, cumin, coriander, anise, okra, brinjals [eggplant], pomegranates, oranges, figs—and so up to the plains, where wheat, barley, beans, and lentils of various sorts, with olives and vines, would form the staple products. Gilead especially is essentially a country of wine and oil . . . . [37]

The group continued to Jerusalem and Haifa for brief stops, and then turned their thoughts to a visit with Midhat Pasha, Governor General of Syria and a friend of the Prince of Wales. The scouting party spent three weeks with Midhat in Damascus, who vowed his support for the colonization endeavor. The only two remaining obstacles were the Sultan and the actual Jewish refugees who would be allowed to resettle in Palestine. After several weeks in Constantinople, Laurence was finally summoned for a meeting in April 1880. The Sultan listened attentively to the proposal, and then informed Oliphant that his ministers were against the plan—effectively halting any hope of colonization.

Determined to help Zionist families escape persecution in Russia and Romania, Laurence offered to raise sufficient funds in England to aid their resettlement in Turkey. As a result, he became something of the equivalent of a "rock star" as an advocate for Jews. Unfortunately, his trip to Palestine and subsequent meeting with the Sultan had taken a toll on Laurence's health. As he swayed on the brink of a mental collapse, he received word that Alice, who had apparently heard from friends about his physical and mental frailty, was rejoining him in England. She arrived on November 1, 1880 and informed her mother that she would return home shortly. In short order, Alice developed a cough and Laurence's doctor ordered both husband and wife to a sunnier climate to aid in recovery. Happy to be together once again, the pair set sail for Egypt.

Even as the two enjoyed the adventures of a delayed vacation, the influence and grip of Thomas Lake Harris was loosening. When challenged with unrealistic demands by Harris, the couple returned to England where Laurence secured a rental cottage at Windsor, near Margaret Oliphant, and there ensconced Alice. She was to remain in England while her husband set sail for America to visit his mother and friends still at one of Harris' compounds. Upon arrival, Laurence demanded the return of the funds that both he and his mother had invested in the cult and its leader. During this trip to the United States, in October 1881, Lady Maria Oliphant died. Before Laurence returned to England, the suit against Harris was settled, leaving Laurence with no reason to ever go back to California.

Arriving back in England in January 1882 for a reunion with Alice—sans Harris—Laurence learned of new brutalities launched against Jews in Eastern Europe. On January 11, 1882, *The Times of London* published explicit particulars of the carnage:

> During the past eight months, a track of country, equal in area to the British Isles and France combined, stretching from the Baltic to the Black Sea, has been the scene of horrors

hitherto only . . . . perpetrated in medieval days during times of war. Men ruthlessly murdered, tender infants dashed to death, or roasted alive in their own homes, married women the prey of brutal lust that has often caused their death, and young girls violated in the sight of their relatives by soldiers who should have been the guardians of their honour.[38]

It presented a new opening for Laurence to lend a helping hand to Jewish people, and perhaps make a difference in a world of rising Jew-hatred. Soon, under the auspices of the Mansion House Committee, established to aid suffering Jews, Alice and Laurence were dispatched to categorize according to their abilities those who had escaped from Eastern Europe. After being catalogued, the refugees were selected for possible emigration to Palestine—especially those who were able to farm, work on machinery, or provide necessary labor in agricultural settings.

The Oliphants were thrilled with the opportunity. Margaret Oliphant visited with them before their departure and wrote:

They were all packed and ready for their start, not knowing precisely where Providence might lead them before they came back, but facing all the hazards of the future with a pleasant confidence—a confidence, no doubt, springing from an over sanguine and buoyant nature, but chiefly from the sense of the great work which they felt to be in their hands, and which they were sure of the guidance of God to enable them.[39]

The couple went first to Paris, then to Berlin where they met with British Ambassador, Odo Russell, and the Crown Prince and Princess of Prussia. Both parties expressed support for their undertaking. After several months of stops in the snowy and icy part of northern Europe, Alice and Laurence stopped in Constantinople. Alice's letters reveal her joy in the stopover:

> "This is a lovely spot," Mrs. Laurence writes to her sister, "as indeed every spot along the Bosphorus seems to be; and we have chosen rooms in a house that is a little way up the abrupt slope . . . . which enables us to look up and down the Straits from our windows."[40]

In the meantime, Laurence had made arrangements with

the overseer of the land he was awarded from Thomas Lake Harris in Brocton, New York, to house forty Jewish refugees. He wrote special instructions to his manager:

> All the first year's expenses will have to be bourne [sic] by our property before their labour can begin to make them independent. We gave orders to have their Sabbaths and all food and special observances respected, of course.[41]

It was while the Oliphants were in Constantinople that they met Naphtali Herz Imber, a young Jewish man whom they engaged as their secretary. Imber later penned a poem that became the lyrics for the Jewish National Anthem, *Hatikvah*, "The Hope." Soon after the poem surfaced, American composer Sammy Cahn wrote the music for the first nine stanzas. Its popularity quickly grew to legendary proportions. It was included as part of the stirring soundtrack of the film, "Exodus," based on the book of the same name by Leon Uris.

"Hatikvah" was adopted as the official song at the Fifth Zionist Congress in 1933—along with the blue and white Star of David as the emblem of Jews in Palestine. Imber readily agreed that the song would have not been birthed without the staunch support of Alice and Laurence. Although revered by many Israelis and popularly known as the country's national anthem, "Hatikvah" did not become officially designated as such until November 10, 2004.[42] When Imber died in 1909, more than ten thousand gathered to mourn his passing.

The Oliphants landed in Haifa in December 1882, a homecoming of sorts for the two gentiles who had longed to help provide a place for the Jewish people to call home. There they purchased a home from Karl Oldorf, a German settler, where they settled down to the work of enabling Jewish emigration to Palestine. Sadly, the couple who had not been allowed by Harris to spend much time together as husband and wife would not enjoy their later years. On January 2, 1886, after only three short years together, Alice died of complications from malaria. In Paris in 1888, Laurence met Rosamond Dale Owen who was on a visit from the United States. The two seemed well-suited, and as both were intent on aiding Jewish people to resettle in Palestine, they soon boarded a ship for Haifa. While enroute Laurence asked Rosamund to marry him; she accepted his proposal, and they were wed soon after arriving in Palestine. Sadly, only a few days following the wedding, Oliphant began to exhibit signs of illness. He died on December 23, 1888. His good friend, Oswald Smith, who had traveled to Russia with Laurence, wrote:

> Oliphant was never known, as far as my experience goes, to speak unkindly of any one, and so it is, now that he has been taken from us in the prime of his power and influence that there appears to be but one feeling and one language in reference to him. We all grieve that we shall not see that pleasant presence again, that we shall . . . . hear that delightful laugh no more, and that the companionship of which the memory is so sweet, is now a memory and nothing more.[43]

Laurence Oliphant would doubtless be astounded to see the land of Israel today. He would surely gaze in amazement at the fields that produce food, fruits, and flowers; on the cities rising from the desert, and the myriad of peoples from around the world who walk the streets of Jerusalem. Perhaps he would recall the wonder-filled years he and his beloved Alice spent in the Holy Land before death claimed them both. The sanctuary resurrected from the dead sands and rocky outcroppings that time, by all appearances, had forgotten is today the land of Holocaust survivors; of

Ethiopian and Russian Jews brought home to their ancient land. It is a place that every man woman and child who ever uttered the words, "Never again," can call home, thanks to the Herculean efforts of men and women such as Laurence and Alice Oliphant.

WILLIAM BLACKSTONE

What shall be done for the Russian Jews? . . . . Why not give Palestine back to them again? According to God's distribution of nations it is their home, an inalienable possession from which they were expelled by force. Under their cultivation it was a remarkably fruitful land, sustaining millions of Israelites, who industriously tilled its hillsides and valleys. They were agriculturalists and producers as well as a nation of great commercial importance; the center of civilization and religion.[44]

1

When Jewish poetess Emma Lazarus penned the immortal words emblazoned on the pedestal of the Statue of Liberty, Palestine was desert wastelands in the hands of the unfriendly Turks. From 1881 to about 1920, the United States saw its greatest period of immigration, among which were three million Jews from Eastern Europe. It was the time of "America's Open Door and the Great Melting Pot." Welcoming them to America were Lazarus' words:

> Here at our sea-washed, sunset gates shall stand
> A mighty woman with a torch
> Whose flame is the imprisoned lightning,
> and her name
> Mother of Exiles. . . .

"Keep ancient lands your storied pomp," cries she

With silent lips. "Give me your tired, your poor,

Your huddled masses yearning to breathe free,

The wretched refuse of your teeming shore.

Send these, the homeless, tempest-tost to me,

I lift my lamp beside the golden door!"

Jewish immigrants felt that America held much greater promise for them than returning to Palestine. In fact, many Jews in the United States came to view America as *their* Promised Land. They were comfortable with America's graces and felt no need to seek peace elsewhere. This grand sentiment was not without its repercussions, however. As poor Jews from Europe swarmed to America's shores, it not so much *answered* the question of "The Jewish Problem," but brought it to America. Many leaders felt the U.S. could not hold the influx, and that some other resolution would have to be sought.

As a result, Congress in 1921 passed a quota targeting mostly unskilled European workers. Another law enacted that same year limited each country to sending the equivalent of only three percent of its nationals already living in the U.S. in 1910. This law curbed immigration to 357,000 people. Three years later the Johnson-Reed Immigration

Restriction of 1924 reduced this quota to two percent, while also lowering the base year to 1890—when only 150,000 people were allowed to enter. The government's restrictive policy thus cut immigration from 800,000 in 1921 to a mere 23,000 in 1933. Ellis Island's role quickly changed from that of depot to that of a detention center. In 1915, Ellis Island processed 178,000 immigrants; by 1919 that number had fallen to 26,000. Something different would have to be done to solve what was called "the Jewish problem" in Europe. The answer, emphatically, would not be to allow more Jews to enter the United States.

Long before any of this actually began, Christian businessman William Eugene Blackstone stepped forward with his plan for a solution. Born into a Methodist home in upstate Adams, New York in 1841, young William was only eleven years old when he made the decision to become a Christian during a revival at a Methodist church. The next milestone in his life was the beginning of the Civil War. William was denied service as a soldier due to health reasons, but soon turned his attention to working with the U.S. Christian Commission, a group comparable to the American Red Cross. He served as the director of medical services for those injured in the line of duty.

Sarah Lee Smith, the daughter of real estate developer

and philanthropist Philander Smith, caught William's eye, and the two married on June 5, 1866. The couple purchased a home in Oak Park, Illinois, where Blackstone gained success with a construction and investment company. But in time, he reached a point in his life when he began to wrestle with God regarding the direction his life was taking.

After a single night spent in prayer, personal introspection, and spiritual battle, Blackstone made the decision to dedicate his life to service to God. He vowed that he would give two years of his life to missionary work, but it was a pledge that would last a lifetime. He forsook materialistic quests and began to proclaim the gospel. His focus was on the Rapture (or catching away) of the Church, and the return of Christ.

Blackstone had from childhood been an ardent student of the Bible. In 1878, he published the first bestseller on dispensationalism called *Jesus Is Coming!* It sold over a million copies (no small feat in a nation of only about fifty million—roughly a sixth of America's population today), and was translated into thirty-six languages. While the book was offensive to many who had grown comfortable in their American Christianity and were content to live the American dream, it was welcomed by such men as Dwight

L. Moody and Cyrus I. Scofield who appreciated this literal interpretation of the scriptures and welcomed a more active and evangelical, missions-minded Christianity. It so touched the American conscience that it, according to author John Walvoord, "in a large measure set the tone for this period of history."[45]

Of Blackstone's stance on dispensationalism Timothy Weber wrote:

> Most dispensationalists were satisfied to be mere observers of the Zionist movement. They watched and analyzed it. They spoke out in favor of it. But seldom did they become politically involved to promote its goals. There is one exception to the general pattern, however, in the person of William E. Blackstone, one of the most popular dispensational writers of his time.[46]

Blackstone's book was so well documented it was actually more scripture than commentary. Because of limited space, the book listed hundreds of Bible passages for the reader to review on his or her own. It was a book difficult for any true believer to ignore. Once again, an American had become a beacon to enlighten the world to Bible prophecy. The book was eventually translated into forty-eight languages, including Hebrew, and is still in print today.

Chapter fifteen of the book, titled simply, "Israel to Be Restored," starts with this passage:

> Perhaps you say, "I don't believe the Israelites are to be restored to Canaan, and Jerusalem to be rebuilt."
>
> Have you read the declarations in God's Word about it? Surely nothing is more plainly stated in the Scriptures.[47]

From here, Blackstone went on to list eighty-nine different Scripture passages that support this assertion. Later in the chapter he further states:

> It would seem that such overwhelming testimony would convince every fair-minded reader that there is a glorious future restoration in store for Israel. . . .
>
> I could fill a book with comments about how Israel will be restored, but all I have desired to do was to show that it is an incontrovertible fact of prophecy, and that it is intimately connected with our Lord's appearing.[48]

Perhaps Blackstone's remarks seem somewhat overstated to us who were born after the rebirth of Israel as a state, but to those of his time, some six-and-a-half decades before the event, the confidence of his statements was no less than prophetic. Few in America's churches seemed to give any real credence to the possibility that the Jews would ever return to their own land, much less have a state with Jerusalem as its capital. For their part, the Jews overall had little interest in the idea themselves. By the outbreak of World War I, only about 20,000 of the 2.5 million Jews in the U.S. belonged to any type of Zionist organization.[49] American Jews were quite happy where they were.

However, Blackstone looked upon Israel as "God's sundial." He even went so far as to say, "If anyone desires to know our place in God's chronology, our position in the march of events, look at Israel."[50] For Blackstone, it was the next milestone in the river of prophecy.

In what light, then, did American churches interpret the scriptures Blackstone was quoting? How could they have missed the obviousness of these prophecies concerning the rebirth of Israel? They interpreted them as referring to "spiritual Israel"—as the Church of the modern day. Wisely, Blackstone had a few things to say about this—a subject that would touch on some of the darkest episodes for the descendants of Isaac in the ensuing century. He saw quite plainly that Israel and the Church were separate entities with individual futures as applied to their different covenants. God had not forsaken one for the other, but rather had a unique plan for each.

2

By replacing literal Israel in the Bible with the Church, Christians of that time no longer had to feel any responsibility to the Jews as God's Chosen People. This "Replacement Theology" would be resuscitated to quiet the Church in Germany during World War II, even as the death camps were raised with horrible means of torture and death implemented. No obligation to the Jewish population of Europe was considered. Jews were thought to be "suffering for their sins of rejecting the Messiah." It was as if Jesus' death cut them free from the Hebrew people rather than grafting them into their vine. However they saw it, it was this insidious virus—an invisible moderate anti-Semitism—that allowed the mainstream German Church to look the other way as the most horrific and ungodly things were done.

While attempts in Europe to restore the Jews to a home-land in Palestine were certainly political in nature, budding Restorationism in the United States was largely non-political. The exception was in the political endeavors of William Blackstone. Author Jerry Klinger defined Restorationism in an article for *The Jewish Magazine*:

> Restorationism is the belief derived from direct Biblical interpretation that one of the preconditions for the Second Coming of Jesus was the return of the Jews to their God pledged land of Palestine. Unlike 2,000 years of orthodox Catholic and Eastern Catholic thought that the Jews were replaced by the Church because of their sin of rejecting Jesus, Dispensationalist Christians believe that God had never abandoned his special relationship with the Jewish people.[51]

Blackstone was vocal in his defense of a Jewish homeland and his words did not fall on deaf ears in the United States. As his popularity rose, so did his activity. In 1887, he joined in forming the Chicago Committee for Hebrew Christian Work, which a few years later became the Chicago Hebrew Mission, and still survives today as the American Messianic Fellowship International. In 1888, he and his daughter, Flora, visited Palestine, and concluded their trip in London. The trip took about a year.

When they returned, Blackstone was more zealous than ever toward the cause of reestablishing the state of Israel. Shortly thereafter, the burden of his heart was to initiate a conference between Jews and Christians to discuss this very topic. The "Conference on the Past, Present, and Future of Israel" took place November 24-25, 1890 at the First Methodist Episcopal Church in Chicago. It was attended by some of the best-known Christian and Jewish Leaders of the day.

The assembly passed resolutions of sympathy for the oppressed Jews living in Russia, and copies were forwarded to the Czar and other world leaders. However, Blackstone knew that it was not enough to simply beg mercy from these leaders—the Jews needed a land to call their own within whose borders they could find peace and security. He wanted these world figureheads to grant the Jews permission to return to Palestine and establish just such a state. Out of these meetings came the inspiration for the document that would eventually be known as "The Blackstone Memorial."

His political relationships included Lord Anthony Ashley Cooper, seventh Earl of Shaftesbury who, in England, encouraged Blackstone to use those contacts to further promote a Jewish state. Blackstone gathered 413 signatures of prominent Americans—politicians, churchgoers, a few congressmen, mayors of Chicago, Baltimore, and Philadelphia, John D. Rockefeller, J. P. Morgan, William McKinley (who would later become U.S. president), Cyrus McCormick, Supreme Court Justice Melville Fuller, Hugh L. Grant, mayor of New York City, T. B. Reed, Speaker of the House of Representatives, and Robert R. Hitt, Chairman of the House Committee on Foreign Affairs. Blackstone presented the petition to President Benjamin Harrison and his secretary of state, James G. Blaine. It called for a conference to discuss the possibilities of a Jewish homeland—a first step on the road to a Jewish state—and copies were also sent to heads of every European nation.

President Harrison seemed like a man who would favor Israel as well, since he chose Psalm 121:1-6 as the Scripture upon which he would place his hand as he took the Oath of Office as the twenty-sixth President of the United States:

> I will lift up my eyes to the hills—from whence comes my help? My help *comes* from the LORD, Who made heaven and earth. He will not allow your foot to be moved; He who keeps you

will not slumber. Behold, He who keeps Israel shall neither slumber nor sleep. The LORD *is* your keeper; the LORD *is* your shade at your right hand. The sun shall not strike you by day or the moon by night.

Harrison paid little attention to the petition. The Blackstone Memorial did, however, prompt an encore: In the early 1900s American Christian Zionism found its voice, as it had in Britain in the late 1800s. Blackstone was aptly referred to by some as the "father of Christian Zionism."[52]

The first paragraph of Blackstone's memorial began simply, "What shall be done for the Russian Jews?" and the second, "Why not give Palestine back to them again?"[53] Blackstone entreated:

> According to God's distribution of nations it is their home, an inalienable possession from which they were expelled by force. Under their cultivation it was a remarkably fruitful land, sustaining millions of Israelites, who industriously tilled its hillsides and valleys. They were agriculturalists and producers as well as a nation of great commercial importance--the centre of civilization and religion. Why shall not

the power which under the treaty of Berlin, in 1878, gave Bulgaria to the Bulgarians and Serbia to the Serbians now give Palestine back to the Jews?[54]

The letter that accompanied his memorial ended with these words:

> . . . . there seem to be many evidences to show that we have reached the period in the great roll of the centuries, when the ever-living God of Abraham, Isaac, and Jacob, is lifting up His hand to the Gentiles, (Isaiah 49:22) to bring His sons and His daughters from far, that he may plant them again in their own land, (Ezekiel 34, &c). Not for twenty-four centuries, since the days of Cyrus, King of Persia, has there been offered to any mortal such a privileged opportunity to further the purposes of God concerning His ancient people.
>
> May it be the high privilege of your Excellency, and the Honorable Secretary, to take a personal interest in this great matter, and secure through the Conference, a home for these wandering millions of Israel, and thereby

receive to yourselves the promise of Him, who said to Abraham, "I will bless them that bless thee," Genesis 12:3.[55]

While most Americans today may never have heard of William E. Blackstone, the same could not have been said of American Presidents from William Harrison to Harry Truman. Blackstone believed that the Church could well be raptured[56] at any moment, and became increasingly preoccupied with "God's sun-dial"—the Jewish people and their promised return to Palestine. He kept the issue before the eye of every U.S. president until his death in 1935.

Blackstone not only handed the Memorial to Harrison, but would also see it presented to Presidents William McKinley, Grover Cleveland, Theodore Roosevelt, and Woodrow Wilson—William McKinley even signed it.[57] Blackstone's words so saturated these presidents, that in 1949, some fourteen years after Blackstone's death, Harry Truman, who made the U.S. the first nation to recognize the newborn state of Israel, quoted Blackstone's letter virtually verbatim. When he was introduced to some Jewish scholars that year as "the man who helped create the State of Israel," Truman responded with, "What do you mean 'helped create'? I am Cyrus, I am Cyrus!"[58] Truman was comparing his actions to that of Cyrus the Great, who in BCE 539 fought and defeated the Babylonians, freeing 40,000 Jewish captives and allowing them to return to the Promised Land.

Blackstone's memorial was written five years before the father of modern-day Zionism, Theodor Herzl, published his book, *The Jewish State* and founded the Zionist Movement. In fact, when Blackstone discovered that Herzl's book was both practical and political, not prophetic, he marked all the prophecies in the Old Testament concerning Israel's rebirth in a Bible, and sent it to Herzl. Blackstone informed Herzl that his proposal to have a Jewish state in Argentina, Uganda, or any other country was unacceptable—it had to be in the promised land of Palestine with Jerusalem as its capital. Blackstone so greatly influenced Herzl that the Bible containing those marked prophecies was once displayed in Herzl's tomb in Israel.

Because of his zeal, Blackstone is perhaps the most famous American in Israel today. While righteous gentiles such as Corrie ten Boom and Oskar Schindler have a tree dedicated to them for saving lives in the Holocaust, Blackstone had a forest named after him and is mentioned in most textbooks discussing the history of Israel.

David Rausch wrote of Blackstone's impact on the Zionism movement:

> Zionism humanly speaking owes its origin not primarily in the Jewish fold, but in the efforts of a Christian, one whom we all respect, and who has been a great friend of Jewish Missions, William E. Blackstone.[59]

Israeli Prime Minister Benjamin Netanyahu also acknowledged the role of Christian Zionism. He wrote that it: "antedates the modern Zionist movement by at least half a century."[60]

Despite his presence before these presidents and his popularity, however, Blackstone would be to these presidents what Moses was to Pharaoh—a voice calling from God, "Let My people go!", but also a plea that—for the most part—would go unheeded. As Pharaoh vacillated in his decision to release the Jews to go to Canaan (ancient Palestine) after the plagues, so would the American presidents. However, it was not God who hardened presidential hearts as He had done with Pharaoh; it would be the State Department.

3

While it had been the State Department that incited U.S. protests against the murder of Jews in Damascus in 1840, it would again be the State Department that would silence U.S. response to Blackstone's plea, and eventually underscored America's apathy towards the murder of six million Jews during the Holocaust. The death knell that sounded over the Blackstone Memorial came in a penciled note from Alvey A. Adee, who was U.S. Assistant Secretary of State from 1886 to 1924, an incredible thirty-eight year stint in the office that left his fingerprints everywhere on America's foreign policy, throughout his tenure and beyond. If Adee felt one way, than it was a good indication of the way any up-and-coming young State Department officer should feel if one hoped for advancement. His note read:

For thirty years and I know not how much longer, Turkey has writhed under the dread of a restoration of the Judean monarchy. Every few months we are asked to negotiate for the cessation of Palestine to the Jewish "nation." The whole project is chimerical.[61]

While, in fact, the project was not the impossible and foolish fancy as Adee suggested, his note was enough to infect the State Department with the idea that any action towards helping Israel become a nation again was not only a waste of time, but also not in the interest of peaceful relations with the powers that controlled the region at the time—namely the crumbling Ottoman Empire. The tone was also set in those intellectual halls that the simplistic, black-and-white values and ideals of Evangelical Christians such as Blackstone were naive and quixotic. It was assumed that well-informed diplomats knew more about the values and cultures of the regions involved, so they were in a better position to make policy regarding the issues concerning them.

A further prophetic insight was realized when William Blackstone's friend, Cyrus Scofield, published his famous study Bible in 1909. It was greatly inspired by Blackstone's interest in Bible prophecy and simple, straightforward interpretation of scripture. In his notes, Scofield interpreted Ezekiel 38 and 39 to mean that Russia would invade Israel during the End Time. That interpretation was challenged and even mocked. Many said, "How can you possibly say that? Russia is a Christian Orthodox nation, and Israel doesn't even exist . . . nor is there any possibility that Israel will exist." Scofield answered simply, "I don't understand it, and I can't explain it, but the Bible says it, and I believe it." Today no one doubts that Russia might attack Israel—especially since it has been known to regularly aim nuclear missiles at cities in Israel—and Scofield's interpretation is usually taken for granted.

William Blackstone was God's voice to his generation. He had raised the call for Zionism even before The Zionist Movement was founded. Through Blackstone, God was calling on the conscience of the America that had called on Him to save it from the tyranny of the British, and then save it from divisive internal strife over the issue of slavery. God answered willingly and faithfully, keeping America whole through each of these as well as other conflicts. Now God was calling on America to act on behalf of His chosen people, the Jews—and for more than fifty years, His call was ignored. The fact of the matter is, had any of the presidents who received Blackstone's Memorial acted upon it—in other words, if they had acted on prophecy instead of disregarding it—it might well have saved the lives of the six million Jews who died in the Holocaust as well as the lives of those persecuted in Russia and elsewhere in the world. It has been said that America's inaction during this time was as responsible for the Holocaust as the silence of the German Church in the 1930s and 40s.

The fulfillment of prophecy concerning God's people has never been a unilateral act of God. First, God informs His prophets what is to come to pass (which can mean quickening His Scriptures to them as happened with Daniel), then His people begin to pray, and God moves on the hearts of leaders to fulfill His word concerning these things. This seems exactly the pattern that occurred with William Blackstone and the leaders of his day. Blackstone understood what biblical prophecy said, he and others began to pray over it, and suddenly leaders all over the world began to pick up their standards in support. As the U.S., England, and the rest of Europe directed global politics at that time, so these nations were in the thick of fulfilling the prophecies Blackstone had recounted.

Associate Supreme Court Justice Louis D. Brandeis was unparalleled in shaping President Woodrow Wilson's Zionist leanings. When in 1916 he remembered having read the Blackstone Memorial, Brandeis sent for its author. He had his friend and intercessor, Nathan Straus, write a letter to Blackstone on his behalf. It read, in part:

> Mr. Brandeis is perfectly infatuated with the work that you have done along the lines of Zionism. It would have done your heart good to have heard him assert what a valuable contribution to the cause your document is. In fact he agrees with me that you are the Father of Zionism, as your work antedates Herzl.[62]

Brandeis asked Blackstone to recirculate a modern-day version of his Memorial in order to deliver it to President Wilson.

As the son of a Presbyterian minister, Wilson had always sensed God's hand upon him for the purpose of doing great good. For the Scripture upon which he would place his hand to take the Oath of Office in 1917, Wilson had chosen:

> The heathen raged, the kingdoms were moved: he uttered his voice, the earth melted. The Lord of hosts is with us; the God of Jacob is our refuge. Selah. (Psalm 46:6, 11)

Britain's ambassador at that time, Sir Cecil Spring-Rice,

had in fact noted this, stating that "He believes God sent him here to do something." Peter Grose, author of *Israel in the Mind of America*, had this to say about Wilson's support of the idea:

Finally, the prophetic stream of Christian thought had its effects on Wilson, with his daily Bible readings, his romantic visions of the people of the Book. The evangelist Blackstone, undeterred by the lack of interest of previous presidents, persisted in his campaigns for the Jewish State; in 1916 he persuaded the Presbyterian General Assembly, governing body of Wilson's own church, to endorse the Zionist goal. "To think that I, the son of the manse, should be able to help restore the Holy Land to its people," Wilson once remarked. In October 1918 British Prime Minister Lloyd George wanted to be certain that the United States stood with Britain on the matter of the Balfour Declaration. In a letter to Rabbi Stephen Wise, President Wilson wrote:

I welcome the opportunity to express the satisfaction I have felt in the progress of the

Zionist movement in the United States and the Allied countries since the declaration of Mr. Balfour on behalf of the British Government, of Great Britain's approval of the establishment in Palestine of a national home for the Jewish people, and his promise that the British Government would use its best endeavors to facilitate the achievement of that object . . . . [63]

In 1918 a Zionist Conference in Philadelphia acclaimed Blackstone a founding 'Father of Zionism,' and in 1956, on the seventy-fifth anniversary of Blackstone's Memorial to President Harrison, the citizens of the state of Israel dedicated a forest in his honor.[64]

In 1918 William Blackstone was honored by Elisha M. Friedman, University Zionist Society of New York. Friedman said of Blackstone:

A well-known Christian layman, William E. Blackstone, antedated Theodor Herzl by five years in his advocacy of the re-establishment of a Jewish State . . . . After traveling to Europe, Egypt, and Palestine in 1888, Blackstone [with his own funds] organized in Chicago in 1890 one of the first conferences between Christians and Jews [the Conference on the Past, Present and Future of Israel]. The Jews of Russia were being persecuted and William Blackstone felt that mere resolutions of sympathy were inadequate."[65]

William Blackstone maintained contact with both Nathan Straus and Mr. Justice Brandeis until his death. The dedicated Zionist had spent 57 years as a champion of Zionism and the Jewish people. Klinger noted:

[Blackstone] spoke out actively and aggressively against anti-Semitism focusing in particular on the hatred spread by Henry Ford in his advocacy for the *Protocols of the Elders of Zion*.[66]

God sent men like William Blackstone to help save the children of Israel from anti-Semitic hatred; but president after president ignored him. He sent the prosperity of the 1920s to show He loved us, but we still didn't listen, so He sent the depression as a final attempt to inspire us to "call on His Name, humbling ourselves and praying, seeking His face, and turning from our wicked ways." But we did not. Thus it was that the world turned its back on the Jews, and Hitler's genocidal extermination machine quickly closed in on them. Regrettably, no one acted to help until it was too late. A third of the world's Jewish population was murdered.

As both Hitler and Roosevelt took power in 1933, it is important to see the position the United States was in *vis-à-vis* the world at that time. William Blackstone was still alive and vocal (he would pass away in 1935), and this would mark the forty-second year that U.S. presidents had Blackstone's Memorial calling for the return of Palestine to the Jews presented to them. America had been through two wars (The Spanish-American War and World War I), had experienced one of its greatest times of prosperity in the 1920s (a ray of hope that had come after the Wilson years) and was plunged into its deepest economic failures in the Great Depression. Franklin Delano Roosevelt would be the tenth president to have the opportunity to respond to Blackstone, but as with the others before him, he would not. He would also be the last U.S. president who could have taken action to prevent the Holocaust. Yet even into the middle of the war, when over three million Jews had already been executed, F.D.R. still remained eerily silent on the matter. It appears that perhaps America's greatest Democratic president was also part of our darkest hour as a nation in relating to the children of Israel.

WILLIAM HECHLER

Yesterday, Sunday afternoon, I visited the Rev. Hechler.
Next to Colonel Goldsmid, he is the most unusual person
I have met in this movement so far. He lives on the
fourth floor; his windows overlook the Schillerplatz.
Even while I was going up the stairs I heard the sound
of an organ. The room which I entered was lined with
books on every side, floor to ceiling. Nothing but Bibles.

—THEODOR HERZL [67]

1

Wiliam Henry Hechler became one of the most prominent Christian Zionists and restorationists of his day. For over thirty years he worked diligently to help the Jews realize their goal of establishing a Jewish state in the land of Palestine. He was present in Basle, Switzerland at the First Zionist Congress, where the foundation for his dream, and the dream of so many others, was laid.

William was born in Benares, India, on January 10, 1845 to German Anglican missionary parents Dietrich and Catherine Cleeve Palmer Hechler. William's mother died in 1850, when he was only five years old. Dietrich then sent his son to schools in England and Switzerland. William proved to be smart, spirited, and especially sensitive in the study of religion. He excelled in language skills, and incredibly added Latin, German, Italian, Spanish, Portuguese, French, Hebrew, Greek, Arabic, and two African dialects to his native English tongue.

Dietrich's studies of the writings of those who had developed the theology of Restorationism, deeply influenced his son. He read the works of men such as author Carl Ehle who wrote that Restorationism was not encouraged during medieval times.[68] Among those who opposed that teaching and spoke positively about the Jews returning to Palestine was Gerard of Borgo San Donnino. He lectured that during the End Times Jews would be drawn back to their homeland, and was the rare exception, as most medieval Europeans were rabidly anti-Semitic.[69]

There were, however, early Christian gentiles dating back to the 1600s and 1700s who were determined to aid the Jews. Pamphlets and booklets about end-time theology began to appear in Europe among the Dutch Calvinists, French Huguenots, and the reform movement in the Lutheran Church in Germany. The Puritans of England were among the first to espouse the doctrine of Restorationism in Britain. Author and historian Barbara Tuchman wrote, "Starting with the Puritan ascendancy, the movement among the English for the return of the Jews to Palestine began."[70] Puritans were not only nonconformists but also a Protestant sect that cherished the Old Testament teachings to an extraordinary measure. According to Tuchman:

> They began to feel for the Old Testament a preference that showed itself in all their sentiments and habits . . . . They baptized their children by the names not of Christian saints but of Hebrew patriarchs and warriors. They turned the weekly [service] into the Jewish Sabbath. They sought for precedents to guide their ordinary conduct in the books of Judges and Kings.[71]

Francis Kett was among those in England who proposed that the Jews be allowed to return to their land. He was a scholarly man educated at Cambridge. As early as 1585 Kett published *The Glorious and Beautiful Garland of Mans Glorification Containing the Godly Misterie* [sic] *of Heavenly Jerusalem*—a cumbersome title at best. In his tome, he wrote of "the notion of Jewish national return to Palestine."[72] Kett was subsequently labeled a heretic for his biblical views, and on January 14, 1589, tragically met his death by being burned at the stake.

In the early 1600s, a number of books were written by various Zionists advocating Restorationism. Among them were *The Worldes Resurrection: On the general calling of the Jews, A familiar Commentary upon the eleventh Chapter of Saint Paul to the Romaines, according to the sense of Scripture,* by Thomas Draxe, published in 1608, and *A Revelation of The Revelation,* by Thomas Brightman, in 1609. Another major advocate of the return of the Jews to Palestine was British minister Reverend Henry Finch. His was, perhaps, the first definitive proposal for restoration. In 1621, he wrote *The World's Resurrection or The Calling of the Jewes. A Present to Judah and the Children of Israel that loyned [joined] with Him, and to Ioseph [Joseph] (that valiant tribe of Ephraim) and all the House of Israel that loyned [joined] with Him*—another title of unimaginable length. Britain's King James was not amenable to Finch's interpretation of Scripture; he had both Finch and his publisher arrested. They were examined by a tribunal, whereupon the author was stripped of his position and standing. He died soon after this ordeal.[73]

In 1642, a book by English biblical scholar Joseph Mede, *The Key of the Revelation,* was printed. It was followed in 1639 by Thomas Goodwin's *An Exposition of the Book of Revelation.* In his writings, Goodwin taught that the Jews would become Christians by 1656.[74] Many who adopted Goodwin's theory believed in Jewish restoration as well. Giles Fletcher, Queen Elizabeth I's ambassador to

Russia, was also an advocate of Restorationism and wrote the long-titled treatise *Israel Redux: or the Restauration of Israel, Exhibited in Two Short Treatises.*

During the seventeenth century Puritan religionists in Great Britain continued to teach Restorationism. One of the most vocal was John Owen, a nonconformist church leader and theologian. He penned, "The Jews shall be gathered from all parts of the earth where they are scattered, and brought home into their homeland."[75] In 1790, Richard Beere, a rector in the Anglican Church, sent a letter to Prime Minister William Pitt the Younger to encourage support for a move to restore the Jews to their homeland. Beere was convinced that the official had been sent by God "for such a time as this."[76]

The list of Europeans who contributed to the restoration movement and argued for a Jewish homeland in Palestine is long. It includes such men as Isaac de la Peyrere, who wrote in *Du Rappel des Juifs* (return or recall of the Jews) in 1643 that "the Jewish people, since they were the first to be elected by God, will one day be recalled to the Holy Land, and re-established as the children of God."[77] From England alone came restorationists John Milton (*Paradise Lost*), John Bunyan (*Pilgrim's Progress*), Roger Williams (founder of Providence, Rhode Island, in America), Oliver

Cromwell (Lord Protector of the Commonwealth), and John Sadler, Cromwell's private secretary. Under Cromwell, the Jews who had been expelled from Great Britain in 1290 were invited in 1656 to return. According to the Cromwell Association website, Cromwell's intentions may have been less than altruistic for two very distinctive reasons:

> There was interest in Jewish matters in the leadership of the Commonwealth and Protectorate for two reasons, one pragmatic and the other doctrinal. The pragmatic reason was that based on the international trade and commercial connections of the Amsterdam Jewish community it was recognized that a strong Jewish presence in London would be advantageous. With flourishing links to the East and West Indies and to the New World Jewish traders in London could make the city to Amsterdam as a commercial centre.
>
> The doctrinal reason was the belief amongst godly Protestants, including Cromwell, that the conversion of the Jews to Christianity was essential before Christ would return to reign

on earth. 1656 was thought by some to be the actual year in which this would happen.[78]

Hechler was also influenced by another individual who favored allowing the Jews to return to the Holy Land, John Toland, an Irishman who frequently debated the subject of theology and politics. He railed against the ghettos into which the Jews were forced to live in Europe and even published a pamphlet entitled, "Reasons for Naturalizing the Jews in Great Britain and Ireland on the Same Footing with All Other Nations." While it didn't have a succinct title, the booklet was seen as the prototype of the civil rights movement—for Jews. Toland championed the Jews of the ghettos in many European countries. It was not until banker and politician Lionel de Rothschild was admitted to the House of Commons in 1866 that the Jews had any official status in England.

Writer and theologian Holeger Paulli of Denmark, a member of the Lutheran reform movement, believed that since the apostle Paul had written of the Messiah's return to Zion, the Jews had to be restored to Palestine as a precursor of Christ's second coming. He believed the so-called Christian nations of Europe should launch a crusade to wrest Palestine from the Muslim rulers and restore it to its "rightful owners, the Jews."[79] Paulli dispatched letters to Dutch King William III, who then ruled England. Appealing to the ego of the monarch, Paulli suggested that such a move would place William in the same category as Cyrus, the Persian king in the Old Testament. For reasons of his own, William III refused to rise to the challenge.

The Marquis de Langallerie of France was among other early Zionists. He hatched a plan to remove the Pope from his position of authority and offer the Holy See in exchange for allowing the Jews to return to Palestine. Perhaps in payment for this scheme, the inventive Langallerie was convicted of high treason and died a year after being incarcerated.[80]

In 1771, *Observations upon Prophecies Relating to the Restoration of the Jews* was published by the clergyman Joseph Eyre. In his treatise, he brought public awareness to the land grant given to Abraham by God. Eyre wrote of the many scriptures of Ezekiel 36 and 37 that recount the Valley of Dry Bones, a prophecy of Israel's resurrection, restoration, and return to the Land of Israel. It was a subject of which Bible-believing Christians and Jews of the Diaspora had for centuries spoken. Eyre was certain the children of Israel—a people with an innate desire to return to the Holy Land—would be gathered from the lands from wherever they had been scattered.

A Spanish Jesuit also played a role in the advent of Christian Zionism. Manuel Lacunza, under the nom de plume Juan Josafat Ben-Ezra, wrote *The Coming of the Messiah in Glory and Majesty*. Lacunza claimed to have been a Jew who had accepted Jesus Christ as the Messiah. His work influenced Edward Irving, who wholeheartedly embraced Lacunza's idealistic theory regarding the apocalyptic events predicted to precede the return of the Messiah. Irving learned the Spanish language in order to translate the Jesuit's work into English.[81]

Subsequently, Lacunza was so influenced by Irving that he added 203 pages to the original text expounding on the End Times, prophesying the apostasy of the Church, the rebirth of Israel, and the return of the Messiah. Irving's observations and beliefs deeply impacted such men as John Nelson Darby (about whom more is written later) and Henry Drummond. Drummond and Irving later founded the Catholic Apostolic Church.

During the eighteenth century Christian Zionists were also known as Restorationists. The faction was comprised chiefly of politicians, writers, and theologians. Among the most distinguished was the Bishop of Bristol, Thomas Newton. He battled anti-Semitism while preaching that the Jews would someday return to their homeland. The movement spread as a result of the revolution in France and Napoleon's far-flung battles. Newton was noted for a quote regarding the Jewish people. He said:

> The preservation of the Jews is really one of the most signal and illustrious acts of Divine Providence . . . . and what but a supernatural power could have preserved them in such a manner as none other nation upon earth hath been preserved. Nor is the providence of God less remarkable in the destruction of their enemies, than in their preservation . . . . We see that the great empires, which in their turn subdued and oppressed the people of God, are all come to ruin . . . . And if such hath been the fatal end of the enemies and oppressors of the Jews, let it serve as a warning to all those, who at any time or upon any occasion are for raising a clamor and persecution against them.[82]

Hechler, greatly influenced not only by his father, but by these men and other restorationists, began to delve deeply into the philosophy and to develop his own studies of the End Times and a projected timeline for the return of Christ. After his schooling had been completed in 1870, William joined the German army as a minister and medic during the Franco-Prussian War. He was a decorated soldier, having served with merit and been wounded twice during the duration of the short conflict.

When the war ended in 1871, William was posted to Lagos, Nigeria as a missionary. Malaria proved to be his downfall, prompting the return to Germany to recuperate at his father's home in Karlsruhe where Dietrich worked with Jews. Fully restored to health in 1873, William was recruited as tutor in the home of Frederick I, Grand Duke of Baden. It was in that setting that Hechler established a friendship with the man who would become Kaiser Wilhelm II. It was, in fact, his Restorationism observations and beliefs that would draw the two men together.

After the untimely death of Frederick's son, Prince Ludwig, William was posted to County Cork in Ireland. There, he met Henrietta Huggins, the young lady who would become his wife and bear him four children—Hannah, Amy Victoria, Ludwig Ernest, and Miriam Ada. In 1879, William was summoned to London to become a prelate in the Church of England.

2

In 1881, Hechler was promoted to the post of Metropolitan Secretary of the Church Pastoral Aid Society. It was an opportune appointment for a young man whose interests lay in both Jewish issues and Restorationism. This afforded William the opportunity for travel to Russia, Germany, and France to scrutinize treatment of Jews in those countries. It was in Russia that he ran headlong into brutal pogroms launched against Jewish inhabitants. It was also in Odessa that he was introduced to Leon Pinsker.

In 1882, Pinsker, a contemporary of Theodor Herzl, wrote an essay entitled "Auto-Emancipation." The dissertation intimated that the Jews would never rival the gentiles in social rank as long as they had no country of their own. He wrote:

This is the kernel of the problem, as we see it: the Jews comprise a distinctive element among the nations under which they dwell, and as such can neither assimilate nor be readily digested by any nation . . . . Hence the solution lies in finding a means of so readjusting this exclusive element to the family of nations, that the basis of the Jewish question will be permanently removed . . . . nations live side by side in a state of relative peace, secured by treaties and international law . . . . it is different with the people of Israel. There is no such equality in the nations' dealings with the Jews. The basis is absent upon which treaties and international law may be applied: mutual respect. Only when this basis is established . . . . can the Jewish problem be considered solved . . . . To sum up then, to the living the Jew is a corpse, to the native a foreigner, to the homesteader a vagrant, to the proprietary a beggar, to the poor an exploiter and a millionaire, to the patriot a man without a country, for all a hated rival . . . . We are a flock scattered over the whole face of the earth, and no shepherd to protect us and bring us together . . . . The proper, the only solution, is in the creation of a Jewish nationality, of a people living upon its own soil, the auto-emancipation of the Jews; their return to the ranks of the nations by the acquisition of a Jewish homeland.[83]

Pinsker's plea for a meeting of Jewish leaders to discuss a Jewish homeland was ultimately resolved by Herzl's push for just such an event. During the First Zionist Congress, Pinsker headed the *Hovevei Tzion* (Lovers of Zion) organization, which had been formed in Russia. Hechler was thrilled to discover that Jews in the region had a developing desire to return to their homeland. After a brief stop in England, Hechler journeyed to Constantinople where he presented the British Ambassador with a letter from Queen Victoria. She had ordered that the letter be delivered to the Sultan. Offering a solution to the problem of anti-Semitism, the monarch indicated that the Sultan should consider allowing Jews to return to Palestine. The ambassador tersely refused the Queen's request.

A discourse titled, "The Restoration of the Jews to Palestine" was penned by Hechler in 1884. He fervently believed that loving God's chosen people was a Christian duty, and that Jewish people need not be persuaded to embrace Christianity before Christ's return.

William's dream of a post in Jerusalem was realized when he was sent there as Bishop at Christ Church. In 1885, he authored a superior history of the Protestant church in Palestine entitled, *The Jerusalem Bishopric*, in an attempt to gain the position he so desired.

As a sign of his commitment to the restoration of the Jewish people to their homeland, he included in the book the words to "For Zion's Sake I Will Not Rest," a hymn based on Isaiah 62, and written by British poet John Quarles:

> For Zion's sake I will not rest
> I will not hold my peace
> Until Jerusalem be blest
> And Judah dwell at ease;
>
> Until her righteousness return
> As daybreak after night—
> The lamp of her salvation burn
> With everlasting light.
>
> The Gentiles shall her glory see,
> And kings declare her fame;
> Appointed unto her shall be
> A new and holy name.

The watchmen on her walls appear,

And day and night proclaim,

Zion's deliverer is near;

Make mention of His name.

The Lord upholds her with His hand,

And claims her for His own—

The diadem of Judah's land

The glory of His crown.

Go through, go through, prepare the way,

The gates wide open fling;

With loudest voice let heralds say,

Behold thy coming king![84]

Hechler was crushed when communications between England and Prussia forestalled his appointment as Bishop of Jerusalem. His frustration contributed to an already growing strain with his spouse and led to the failure of his marriage that same year. Despite his disappointment, he accepted a post as Chaplain in the British Embassy in Vienna, and served in that capacity until 1910. Why was this important? While wandering through bookstalls in March 1896, William sighted a book titled *The Jewish State* (*Der Judenstaadt*), by noted Austrian writer, Theodor Herzl. The author proffered what he thought to be a simple resolution to the issue of anti-Semitism: allow Jews to return to their ancient homeland. Hechler purchased Herzl's book and was quickly taken by its contents. The eccentric and full-bearded preacher later met and bonded with Herzl, whom he considered to be a messianic figure. Herzl wrote of his first meeting with Hechler:

> The Rev. William H. Hechler, chaplain to the British Embassy in Vienna, called on me. A likeable, sensitive man with the long grey beard of a prophet. He waxed enthusiastic over my solution. He, too, regards my movement as a "prophetic crisis"—one he foretold two years ago.[85]

Herzl added:

> Yesterday, Sunday afternoon, I visited the Rev. Hechler. Next to Colonel Goldsmid, he is the most unusual person I have met in this movement so far. He lives on the fourth floor; his windows overlook the Schillerplatz. Even while I was going up the stairs I heard the sound of an organ. The room which I entered was lined with books on every side, floor to ceiling. Nothing but Bibles.[86]

Hechler was invited by Herzl to attend the inaugural Zionist Congress in Basel, Switzerland, and was designated by Herzl as the "first Christian Zionist." Because of his contacts with the family of Kaiser Wilhelm II, William worked diligently to secure an audience for Herzl with the monarch. He was able to petition another former student, the wife of the German ambassador, to arrange a meeting with her husband. Although the meeting was held, the Kaiser was unable to persuade his counterpart, the Sultan of Turkey, to permit the Jews to return to Palestine.

Even so, Hechler and Herzl continued to work diligently to promote the Zionist movement, Hechler relentlessly assuring Herzl that his desire for a Jewish homeland was a fulfillment of biblical prophecy.[87]

In his diary, Herzl described Hechler in rather arcane terms:

> Hechler is at all events a curious and complicated character. He is given to pedantry, undue humility, and much pious rolling of the eyes; but, on the other hand, he counsels me superbly, and with unmistakably genuine good-will. He is at once shrewd and mystical, cunning and naïve . . . . His advice and precepts have been

consummate; and unless it turns out later that in one way or another he is a double-dealer, I would wish the Jews to show him a full measure of gratitude.[88]

3

W illiam Hechler gathered a group of Christian Zionists for the express purpose of aiding Russian Jews to escape the pogroms and resettle in Palestine. Along with other colleagues in the Zionist cause, he published a book which he titled, *The Restoration of the Jews to Palestine According to Prophecy.*[89]

Because of his role as tutor to German royalty and to the Grand Duke of Baden in particular, Hechler was instrumental in coordinating a meeting in Palestine between Herzl and Kaiser Wilhelm II to introduce the discussion of a Jewish homeland.[90] He also encouraged the Turkish head of state to contemplate the restoration of a Jewish state.

According to Hermann and Bessi Ellern, who later founded the Association of Jewish Refugees:

[Hechler] regards Herzl as an instrument in the hands of Divine Providence, unfaltering though modest in fulfilling his role, though he himself is unaware of his part in the divine plan.

It was upon this basis that there developed between the Grand Duke and Herzl a relationship, which ascended into the lofty spheres of universal benevolence, to which indeed it returned after every political setback. Because of his status as a quasi-prophetic messenger Hechler would intervene again and again even when Herzl, because of his pride and his desire not to be regarded as a troublesome Jew, hesitated to do so.[91]

In letters from Kaiser Wilhelm II to the Duke of Baden, Hechler wrote with surprising candor:

[The emperor's] attitude towards the Jewish question and Zionism was coloured by anti-Jewish sentiments. In his biography, we learn of the close ties he maintained for some time with the Court Chaplain Adolf Stoecker, author of the anti-Jewish Christian-Social Movement. Here . . . . we are able to see the entire complex of the Emperor's feelings and thoughts on this problem in their proper context.

In his letter to the Duke, too, there is an undertone of popular anti-Semitism. The Emperor [Wilhelm II] wrote that the settlement project would serve to divert "the energy, creativity and practical ability of the tribe of Shem into more honourable channels than battening on the Christians, and that more than one Semite inciting the opposition and belonging to the Social Democrats, will go eastwards to find a more remunerative task, at the end of which there is not—as in the above case—a prison."

He was aware, the Emperor continued, that if it were known "that I regard the Zionists with sympathy and that I am ready—if I were asked by them—even to take them under my protection" the fact would evoke surprise and even opposition among the German people.[92]

In a letter to the Grand Duke dated March 26, 1886, Hechler included a lengthy description of prophecies from both the Old and New Testaments that he felt corroborated his case. He added, "The return of the Jews would become a great blessing to Europe, and put an end to the anti-Semitic spirit of hatred, which is most detrimental to the welfare of all our nations."[93]

So persuasive was Hechler in his dealings with the Kaiser that Wilhelm II acknowledged:

> I have been able to notice that the emigration to the land of Palestine of those Jews who are ready for it is being prepared extremely well and is even financially sound in every respect. Therefore I have replied to an inquiry from the Zionists as to whether I wished to receive a delegation of them in audience that I would be glad to receive a deputation in Jerusalem on the occasion of our presence there. I am convinced that the settlement of the Holy Land by the financially strong and diligent people of Israel will soon bring undreamt-of prosperity and blessing to the land.[94]

Hechler's dream was large and all-encompassing. He had worked meticulously on a set of maps depicting the future State of Israel. He had even included a detailed map of a new Temple in Jerusalem which he believed should be located in Bethel. Through his dealings with Herzl,

Hechler realized that sovereignty for the Jews would come through both political and religious avenues. He ascertained quickly that Herzl would be an instrumental figure in succeeding with a Zionist state and threw his support to his friend.[95]

It was said of Reverend William Henry Hechler that not only was he "the first, but [he was] the most constant and the most indefatigable of Herzl's followers."[96] His contacts both on the continent and in Great Britain were most advantageous to Herzl. Hechler frequently scheduled appointments with the top echelon of German and British leaders, all the while encouraging Herzl that they were "fulfilling prophecy." Hechler said of Lloyd George and Arthur Balfour that they "accepted Zionism for religious and humanistic reasons; they saw it as fulfillment of the Biblical prophecies, not just as something suiting British Imperial interests."[97] Herzl "grew to trust Hechler more and more. Indeed, frequently, for brief but crucial periods, [Herzl] virtually entrusted the entire Zionist enterprise to Hechler, and, though Hechler frequently annoyed and embarrassed him, he never failed him."[98]

Hechler, through his own writings, gives us insight into why he felt he and Herzl were fulfilling prophecy. He wrote:

Every detail of this remarkable Movement
is of interest to us . . . . clergy, who stand as
watchmen on the spiritual walls of Zion . . . .
We are now seeing the stirrings of the bones in
Ezechiel's (sic) valley: Oh! May we soon see the
glorious outpourings of spiritual life predicted
in Ezechiel 36 . . . . The religious element is,
according to God's Word, to become the inspir-
ing force, and, I think I can see that it is the
religious faith in Zionism, which is now already
influencing the whole nation of the Jews . . . .
What food for reflection to every thoughtful
student of the Bible and of history! The Jews
are beginning to look forward to and believe in
the glorious future of their nation when, instead
of being a curse, they are once more to become
a blessing to all.[99]

Prior to his death, Theodor Herzl pressed his case that
Hechler be honored for all he had done for him and the
cause of Zionism. He wrote in his diary, "I would want the
Jews to show him a full measure of gratitude."[100] The Zionist
Organization agreed and rewarded Hechler with a monthly
pension. The day before Herzl died his friend Hechler was

one of the last people to visit him at a sanatorium in Austria. French Presbyterian minister Claude Duvernoy wrote of the bond between the two men. Their relationship, he said, was "the friendly confluence of two Zionist streams, one Jewish and the other Christian, marching side-by-side toward the same kingdom and the same Jerusalem."[101]

Years before his death, Hechler had visited with philosopher Martin Buber in Berlin to warn about what Hechler felt was an approaching *Weltkrieg* (world war). One writer described Hechler's dejection:

> His forewarnings grew into an obsession and he made them with increasing frequency until his death in 1931. Tragically, Hechler's predictions were politely dismissed by everyone.[102]

Two short years later, Adolf Hitler would become Chancellor of Germany, thrusting the world into a devastating war, and the Jews into unimaginable horrors.

In 1997, during the one hundredth anniversary of the First Zionist Congress, Alex Carmel, a historian from Israel, appealed for the restoration of the names of men such as William Hechler, Laurence Oliphant and other outstanding Christian Zionists to the annals of Zionist history.

ARTHUR BALFOUR

Lord Balfour was a statesman almost in spite of himself.
By inclination he was the philosopher, the esthete, the
thinker,the cultured gentleman of leisure, spending his life
among the books and music he loved and knew so well.[103]

—(OBITUARY, *NEW YORK TIMES,*
MARCH 20, 1930)

1

The very conservative First Earl of Balfour was a British Member of Parliament from 1874 to 1922, some of the most formative years of the Zionist movement. He served as prime minister of the United Kingdom just after the turn of the century—from July 1902 to December 1905. Both during and after his term in office, he served as leader of the Conservative Party until 1911, and in 1916 was tapped as foreign secretary under David Lloyd George, the post he held until 1919.

Arthur James Balfour was born July 25, 1848, at Whittingehame House in East Lothian, Scotland, the eldest of three boys and five girls born to Lady Blanche Cecil (the sister of the Marquess of Salisbury). He was named Arthur after his godfather, the Duke of Wellington. The boy's father died when Arthur was seven years old; he lost his mother when he was twenty-four. His childhood religious training was his mother's responsibility, and although christened in the Church of England, Balfour attended a local Presbyterian church. He was schooled at Eton and the University of Cambridge, Trinity College, where he was awarded a second class honors degree in moral sciences. Author Barbara Tuchman wrote in her book *The Proud Tower* that Balfour's religious leanings caused his college friends to view him as "a curious relic of an older generation."[104]

In truth, the pursuit of science and philosophy were more encouraged in his home than the pursuit of theology. Nonetheless, the imminent politician would pursue the study of religion and philosophy his entire life. Sir Austen Chamberlain, British statesman and half-brother of Neville, the British prime minister at the onset of World War II, said of Arthur that he had "the finest brain that has been applied to politics in our time."[105]

It was through his mother's training that Balfour developed a lifelong admiration and sympathy for the plight of the Jews. His niece, Blanche Dugdale, wrote in her memoirs:

The problem of the Jews in the modern world seemed to him of immense importance.

He always talked eagerly on this, and I remember in childhood imbibing from him the idea that Christian religion and civilization owes to Judaism an immeasurable debt, shamefully ill repaid.[106]

Balfour and his cousin, May Lyttelton, had fallen in love, but a marriage between the two was not to be. In 1875, May contracted typhus and died—an event that sealed Balfour's domestic future. In later years, he would form a liaison with Mary Wyndham Charteris (Lady Elcho), but chose to remain single. His spinster sister Alice served as the head of Balfour's household.

Following graduation, his uncle Robert Cecil, the Marquess of Salisbury and foreign secretary under Benjamin Disraeli, invited Arthur to serve as his personal assistant. The lethargic pose that Balfour had adopted coupled with his outward frailty had won for him the kind of teasing he was to endure for his lifetime. While at college in Cambridge he was christened "Miss Nancy." In London he was labeled "Miss Balfour." Because his health was so precarious, it was thought by his family that winters in Egypt might be preferable to a political career. He chose politics.

Balfour enjoyed little success as a Member of Parliament, except that he was befriended by Lord Randolph Churchill (father of Winston who would later become prime minister), Sir Henry Drummond Wolff, and Sir John (then Mr.) Gorst. Arthur was bequeathed a place on the Front Bench in Parliament where he failed to deliver a single speech during his first two terms in office. Finally, when he did make it to the speaker's podium, he delivered a ho-hum dissertation on bimetallism—a system founded on coins of monetary exchange that had been in use in Europe during the eighteenth and nineteenth centuries. (It would be a wonderful, sleep-inducing topic for a modern-day filibuster in Congress.) According to Tuchman, "Balfour was careless of facts, unsafe with figures, and memory was not his strong point . . . . Promptness was not one of his virtues and often he would come lounging gracefully in when Questions were almost over."[107]

It was not until his uncle became foreign minister in 1878 that Arthur's star really began to rise in political circles. That year Balfour accompanied Lord Salisbury to the Berlin congress for meetings conducted by Prince Otto von Bismarck following the end of the Russo-Turkish War. For Balfour, it was a hands-on lesson in international relations and the arts of tact and negotiation. Two years later, when his uncle became prime minister, Balfour was named Secretary for Scotland, followed by an appointment as Chief Secretary for Ireland. A snippet of information in the 1911 Encyclopedia Brittanica is most informative. It reads:

> During this period, from 1886-1892, moreover, he [Balfour] developed gifts of oratory which made him one of the most effective of public speakers. Impressive in matter rather than in manner of delivery, and seldom rising to the level of eloquence in the sense in which that quality was understood in a House which had listened to Bright and Gladstone, his speeches were logical and convincing, and their attractive literary form delighted a wider audience than that which listens to the mere politician.[108]

Of the people he represented in Ireland, Balfour said:

> They have great gifts. They have wit, imagination, eloquence, valor; in many respects they are our superiors. But in one respect they are our inferiors and no amount of Gladstonian rhetoric can make them otherwise. They are politically incapable of self-government.[109]

This attitude and his decision to shoot down rioters without compunction earned Arthur little respect from the Irish and placed him in danger of personal harm from those whom he considered his political inferiors. After returning from his post in Ireland, Balfour served as First Lord of the Treasury and leader of the House of Commons. Upon the resignation of his uncle who was then-prime minister, Lord Salisbury, Arthur succeeded him in the office of prime minister.

The new prime minister faced two particular issues: education and tenant land purchases in Ireland. Foreign affairs in England were left to the foreign secretary, Lord Lansdowne, who excelled in negotiating with other nations. He greatly improved relations with France, and narrowly averted a war with Russia. This freed Balfour to deal with domestic matters. He disagreed with the American concept of equality when the two nations met over the establishment of the League of Nations. According to author David Hunter Miller, Balfour called that particular issue a "19th century proposition that he didn't believe was true. He believed that it was true that in a sense all men in a particular nation were created equal, but not that a man in Central Africa was created equal to a European."[110]

Arthur served in that capacity from 1902 until his

resignation in 1905. His was not a government of renown. At the height of his term as prime minister, Balfour was quoted as saying:

> Give me my books, my golf clubs and my lei-
> sure, and I would ask for nothing more. My ideal
> in life is to read a lot, write a little, play plenty of
> golf and have nothing to worry about. If I could
> give up politics without disorganizing things
> or neglecting my duty, I would gladly do so.[111]

The one significant accomplishment during Balfour's tenure in office was negotiation of the alliance with Russia, Japan, and France—the so-called "iron ring" around Germany—that Britain tried to break in the First World War. Balfour's part in the proceedings was probably not as great as that of Theophile Delcasse, a French diplomat and statesman, but it is generally believed to have been important.[112]

2

In 1916, newly selected Prime Minister David Lloyd George tapped Arthur Balfour to serve as his foreign secretary. In January, before Lloyd George had taken office, British representative Sir Mark Sykes and French representative Francois Georges-Picot had concluded an agreement that allocated postwar spheres of influence in the Middle East to their two nations. Britain would supervise Mesopotamia, most of Transjordan, and southern Palestine. France would take southern Turkey, Syria, northern Palestine, and the Mosul area of upper Mesopotamia.

Author Jonathan Schneer wrote of the two negotiators:

> Sykes was a human dynamo, bubbling with enthusiasm, teeming with ideas, easy to like.

Picot was urbane and reserved. Perhaps in this case opposites attracted. The two men developed a working relationship that they preserved for the entire duration of [World War I] . . . . Together Sykes and Picot redrew the Middle Eastern map.[113]

The area around Jerusalem in central Palestine would require special treatment: The Russian Czar exercised a protective role over various Orthodox monasteries and churches; the French had a similar interest in regard to Catholic institutions. The British represented the somewhat smaller Protestant interests in the area, along with the Germans. However, Britain's prime interest had been the Suez Canal. Consequently, each of these countries had its hand in the cookie jar when it came to central Palestine. Prime Minister David Lloyd George was appalled when he learned of the Sykes-Picot agreement. He wanted Britain to be the sole protector of Palestine—all of Palestine.

Sykes had become convinced that a Jewish national presence in Palestine was in the best interests of the British Empire. He was, however, hampered by the agreement he had signed with the French, which he dared not disclose to the Zionists.

Sykes had hinted that the government was not a free agent in the Middle East, that it needed the endorsement of Paris and Rome before it could officially sponsor the Zionist cause. He asked Chaim Weizmann if he and his cohorts would secure the endorsements needed in Europe. Weizmann and his fellow Zionists left for Europe only to find Sykes seemingly at every turn, carefully stage-managing the entire enterprise.

Sykes' plan succeeded. The French gave the Zionists a letter assuring that they were sympathetic to the Zionist cause. A bigger surprise was the cordial welcome from Pope Benedict XV. This is easily explained: The British were preferable to the Russians and their Orthodox Church when it came to who was going to replace the Turks in Palestine.

Schneer also wrote of the pact:

> The Sykes-Picot Agreement is important for the light it casts upon British thinking about the Middle East during World War I but not for what it accomplished—for it never was implemented.[114]

On June 17, 1917, Balfour urged the Zionists to draw up an appropriate declaration. He promised he would submit the document to the cabinet with his endorsement. Ten years earlier, Balfour had wrestled with the political situation of the Jews in Britain. During a campaign speech while seeking election to parliament, he talked of his certainty that the Jews had long been a wronged people:

> My anxiety is simply to find some means by which the present dreadful state of so large a proportion of the Jewish race . . . . may be brought to an end . . . . [He added] if a home was to be found for the Jewish people . . . . it was in vain to seek it anywhere but in Palestine. [115]

In April 1917, as the Ottoman Empire faced collapse and the question of the disposition of its lands in the Middle East rose to the fore, Balfour traveled to the United States for talks with President Woodrow Wilson. He was also eager to meet new Supreme Court Justice Louis Brandeis, who was seen as the head of organized Jewry in the States. Balfour and Brandeis met for an early breakfast, and after pleasantries were exchanged, the two men began to talk of the political turmoil in the Middle East. Possibly lingering in the back of Brandeis' mind was a cablegram that had preceded Balfour's arrival. English Zionist James Rothschild had written to enlist Justice Brandeis' services to secure an endorsement from the president for the establishment of a Jewish homeland in Palestine under a British protectorate.

In May 1917, Brandeis and President Wilson had a lengthy conversation regarding the United States' position on the Palestine situation. It was their first practical discussion about the principles of Jewish national aspirations. Wilson's administration was unwaveringly against any US responsibility for Palestine or any other portion of the crumbling Ottoman Empire. As a devout Christian Zionist, Balfour's encounter with Brandeis was a brilliant move on his part. He had made contact with a Supreme Court justice, a close adviser to the president who was known for his administrative expertise and lofty ethics, and had a deep personal interest in Brandeis' people, the Jews.

Balfour's awareness of Zionism burgeoned in 1917, when he delivered a treatise that ultimately, but perhaps incorrectly, was called the Balfour Declaration. In his discourse, the politician advocated a homeland in Palestine for the Jews. His detractors proclaimed that Balfour's speech was made simply for the American public. Whatever his reason for speaking out, his interest in the Jewish issue was piqued, and his genuineness following World War I was never doubted.

The Declaration was issued on November 2, 1917, just

over a month before Edmund Allenby would take Jerusalem and nineteen years after Theodor Herzl first championed the return of the Jews to Palestine. The rescue of an astonishingly intact Jerusalem only served to emphasize the interest behind the Balfour Declaration, and it provided yet another seeming verification of the approaching Zionist restoration of the Jewish homeland.

In London, Chaim Weizmann's two closest associates, Harry Sacher and Nahum Sokolow, had set to work on a document to be presented to Balfour. Their final version of the paper was given to him. On the following day, a letter was dispatched to Lord Rothschild. It read:

> I have much pleasure in conveying to you, on behalf of His Majesty's Government, the following declaration of sympathy with Jewish Zionist aspirations which has been submitted to, and approved by, the Cabinet.
>
> His Majesty's Government view with favour the establishment in Palestine of a national home for the Jewish people, and will use their best endeavours to facilitate the achievement of this object, it being clearly understood that nothing shall be done which may prejudice the civil and religious rights

of existing non-Jewish communities in Palestine, or the rights and political status enjoyed by Jews in any other country.

I should be grateful if you would bring this declaration to the knowledge of the Zionist Federation.[116]

Out of the interminable negotiations to establish a Jewish homeland a friendship grew between Dr. Weizmann, a Jewish statesman, and Lord Balfour, the British foreign secretary. Balfour was unable to understand why the Jews were insisting that they would only accept Palestine as their permanent homeland. One day, Lord Balfour asked Dr. Weizmann for an explanation. "Mr. Balfour," Weizmann responded, "let's suppose I propose that you replace London with Paris, would you accept?" A surprised Balfour responded, "But, London is ours!" Replied Weizmann, "Jerusalem was ours when London was still a swampland."[117]

Shortly after its delivery, the Balfour Declaration became the putative guideline of Zionist principles for a future state in Palestine. It also became the foundation for the Jewish Agency, a group comprised of both Zionists and non-Zionists. The organization met in Zurich, Switzerland, during the summer of 1929, with the express purpose of generating support for a Jewish homeland.

3

In later years, speculation abounded that Lord Balfour did not actually draft the Declaration that bears his name. Rather, it is surmised that War Cabinet minister, Lord Alfred Milner, was the author. Carroll Quigley, a Georgetown University professor of history, wrote *The Anglo-American Establishment*. Published in 1981 after Quigley's death, the book states:

> This declaration, which is always known as the Balfour Declaration, should rather be called "the Milner Declaration," since Milner was the actual draftsman and was, apparently, its chief supporter in the War Cabinet. This fact was not made public until 21 July 1937. At that time

Major David Ormsby-Gore[118] (Fourth Baron Harlech) speaking for the government in Commons, said, "The draft as originally put up by Lord Balfour was not the final draft approved by the War Cabinet. The particular draft assented to by the War Cabinet and afterwards by the Allied Governments and by the United States . . . and finally embodied in the Mandate, happens to have been drafted by Lord Milner. The actual final draft had to be issued in the name of the Foreign Secretary, but the actual draftsman was Lord Milner."[119]

Milner's actions were perhaps more suited to changing Balfour's missive than writing the entire document that had been proposed by Harry Sacher and Nahum Sokolow. The two men had written that Palestine was "*the* National Home *of* the Jewish people"; Milner changed that clause to "*a* National Home *for* the Jewish people."[120] His wording positioned the Jews as interlopers, not as a people returning to claim their homeland.

Contrarily, a professor of modern history at Aberystwyth University in Wales, William D. Rubenstein, believes that in 1917 Leo Amery, a pro-Zionist politician and assistant secretary in the War Cabinet, wrote the preponderance of the Balfour Declaration.[121]

The importance of the Balfour Declaration lies not in who wrote it, but rather that the covert support of a homeland for the Jews in Palestine was made public; and Arthur Balfour was the one who courageously presented it to the people. The Declaration urged the League of Nations to consign the Palestine Mandate to Great Britain in July 1922. Also, this recognition by the British government lent significant weight to the vision of a homeland for the Jewish people.

Why is this important? Even though support for the Balfour Declaration was significant, the British reneged on their commitment, which pushed back the time when the Jewish homeland in Palestine would be established and would provide a somewhat safer haven for Jews in peril, particularly in Russia and Germany. Thus, the pogroms in the newly formed USSR continued, and there remained an open door for Hitler to exterminate millions of Jewish men, women, and children in Germany.

Nevertheless, prior to Lord Balfour's Declaration, the push for a Jewish homeland was viewed as nothing more than a pipedream, having little hope of acceptance and even less hope of actual fulfillment. Public endorsement by the British government established the Zionist movement as an acceptable and genuine organization. Author Shalom Goldman wrote:

> Lord Balfour, the British foreign secretary, was a firm believer in the divinely ordered restoration of the Jews to their land. The Balfour Declaration of 1917, facilitated by Balfour's Christian Zionist leanings, elicited great enthusiasm from dispensationalist preachers. For, in their thinking, humanity was now approaching the final dispensation, the one in which the world as we know it would end and the redemptive process would begin . . . . Herzl's associate William Hechler was disappointed that the Balfour Declaration was not couched in religious language . . . . Thirty-one years later, fundamentalists saw the establishment of the State of Israel in1948 as a further "sign of the times," a fulfillment of the promise inherent in the events of 1917.[122]

Harold Begbie, writing under the pseudonym of "A Gentleman with a Duster," summed up the personage who was Arthur Balfour thusly:

Little as the general public may suspect it, the charming, gracious, and cultured Mr. Balfour is the most egotistical of men, and a man who would make almost any sacrifice to remain in office. It costs him nothing to serve under Mr. Lloyd George; it would have cost him almost his life to be out of office during a period so exciting as that of the Great War. He loves office more than anything this world can offer; neither in philosophy nor music, literature nor science, has he ever been able to find rest for his soul. It is profoundly instructive that a man with a real talent for the noblest of those pursuits which make solitude desirable and retirement an opportunity should be so restless and dissatisfied, even in old age, outside the doors of public life.[123]

In 1925, Lord Balfour was invited to Jerusalem for the grand opening of Hebrew University on Mount Scopus. The Jews were pleased; the Arabs were angered and offended, having read the Declaration that bore his name. Balfour had to be quickly removed from Jerusalem because an Arab mob threatened his life.

In March 1930, Chaim Weizmann, Balfour's close friend, visited him at Fishers Hill House in Surrey, the home of Gerald, Balfour's brother. It was in his brother's home that Arthur died on March 19. He had eschewed a public memorial, and was quietly buried alongside other family members at Whittingehame. His title passed to Gerald as Arthur had sired no offspring. He was honored in Israel when the village of Balfouria was named for him, along with the Balfour Forest and a plethora of streets, plazas, and squares in Jerusalem. For instance, the Israeli prime minister's residence in Jerusalem sits on the corner of Balfour Street. The people of Israel will forever treasure the Declaration that bears his name as the first step toward the rebirth of the nation of Israel.

DAVID LLOYD GEORGE

It is unlikely that the Jews would have been
able to establish themselves in Palestine
during the three decades after 1918 had it not
been for David Lloyd George. Quite simply,
Israel might never have existed.[124]

1

David Lloyd George, the future Earl of Dwyfor, was born on January 17, 1963 in Chorlton-on-Medlock, Manchester, England. His father, a Welsh educator, died when David was a baby, leaving the family poverty-stricken. David spoke Welsh as a child, and spoke English as a second language. After the death of her husband, Mrs. George moved back to Wales, where she and her children took up residence with her brother, a Baptist minister and shoemaker.

David was taught the Bible by his uncle, Richard Lloyd, who helped fashion his nephew's religious belief system. When he was fourteen, Richard made it possible for young David to pursue law as a career. At age 50, Richard took it upon himself to learn French, at that time a language necessary for the study of law, and then to teach it to David. He also had to see that his nephew learned Latin, another required language. In 1877, the two made the long journey by train to Liverpool where David was to sit for his preliminary exam. On December 8, 1877, he received word that he had been "successful in passing the preliminary examination of the Incorporated Law Society at Liverpool." The first hurdle to becoming a lawyer had been successfully overcome.

David Lloyd George was apprenticed to the law firm of Messrs. Breese, Jones and Cason, in Portmadoc in July 1878. According to author, Frank Owen:

> Portmadoc is a small country town which is also a seaport. It lies about seven miles east of Llanystumdwy, at the mouth of the Glaslyn River that flows down from Snowdon . . . . The offices there of Messrs. Breese, Jones and Cason were, in many ways, a hub of local business . . . . A young lawyer who meant to be a People's Champion could not have studied his profession in a more useful university.[125]

As a young man, David discovered a precept that supposedly had been adopted by Abraham Lincoln. He duplicated the maxim and kept it on his desk. Lincoln had written:

There is a vague popular belief that lawyers are necessarily dishonest. I say vague, because when we consider to what extent confidence and honors are reposed in and conferred upon lawyers by the people, it appears improbable that their impression of dishonesty is very distinct and vivid. Yet the impression is common, almost universal. Let no young man choosing the law for a calling for a moment yield to the popular belief - resolve to be honest at all events; and if in your own judgment you cannot be an honest lawyer, resolve to be honest without being a lawyer. Choose some other occupation, rather than one in the choosing of which you do, in advance, consent to be a knave.[126]

The handsome and romantic Lloyd George was known to be quite a womanizer during his early adult years. He is said to have indulged in numerous affairs before marrying Margaret Owen in 1888. She much preferred living in Wales, but consented to move into #10 Downing Street when Lloyd George was elevated to the position of prime minister. (Earl, Lord Kitchener, who is mentioned later in this text, commented in the early days of World War I that "he tried to avoid sharing military secrets with the Cabinet, as they would all tell their wives, apart from Lloyd George 'who would tell someone else's wife.'"[127])

The union between Margaret and David, though reportedly not a happy one because of George's reputed infidelity, produced five children—Richard, Mair (who died at an early age), Olwen, Gwilym, and Megan. Margaret stood by her man for years, enduring his alleged repeated adulteries. Robert Lloyd George, author and great-grandson of David, wrote of his great-grandmother:

> She was calm, sensible, full of good humour and in many ways the temperamental opposite of Lloyd George, who was highly strung, brilliant but unpredictable . . . . he stood by him throughout his career, even when he was cited in a divorce case. The scandal that could have ended his political career was completely silenced when Maggie appeared with him in the witness box . . . . When she died in 1941 he was heartbroken.[128]

In 1890, Lloyd George won a seat in Parliament at the by-election (or special election) at Caernarvon Boroughs. Apparently his fidelity in the House of Commons outdistanced that of David as a husband. Collectively, he held the seat for a mind-boggling fifty-five years—by means of his cheeky boldness, charisma, cunning, and commanding ability to debate. He earned a place of preeminence in the radical wing of his party, where he vociferously lobbied against the South African War. That stance almost won him a spot on the business end of a noose in a speech against the war in the very conservative city of Birmingham. While at the Birmingham Town Hall, Lloyd George found himself surrounded by supporters of the war. Robert Lloyd George described it as follows:

> The angry mob broke every window in the building and rushed the speaker's platform inside the hall, armed with sticks, bricks, hammers, and knives. Lloyd George was able to make his escape out the back door by putting on a policeman's helmet and uniform . . . . Two others were killed and forty people injured.[129]

When Lord Balfour resigned as prime minister in 1905, incoming Prime Minister Sir Henry Campbell-Bannerman offered Lloyd George the appointment as president of the Board of Trade. It was said that he proved to be credible and capable in that role. While serving in this position

Lloyd George worked at inaugurating the Port of London Act which established the Port of London Authority. He polished his negotiating skills by settling strikes among various labor factions. His career achievements continued to escalate when Herbert Henry Asquith replaced Prime Minister Campbell-Bannerman—who was forced to retire due to ill health—and appointed Lloyd George to the position of Chancellor of the Exchequer.

During his years in the House of Commons, Lloyd George initiated plans for both health and unemployment insurance. It was he who laid the foundations of the British welfare state, as we know it today. He seemed to avoid foreign policy questions and debates, but as Chancellor, he was plunged over the edge into financial difficulties that would be exacerbated by the Great War.

Asquith, although a skillful and well-educated leader, proved to be an unqualified amateur to oversee the World War that broke out in 1914. He knew little of how to organize the enormous needs attached to fighting such a monumental conflict. Wise decisions were sometimes countered by substantial blunders. The choice of Field Marshall Earl Kitchener as war secretary was overshadowed by Kitchener's missteps during the Gallipoli Campaign. It was agreed by Allied leaders that a sea lane between Russia and the Mediterranean was needed. Thus, a campaign was launched to open that throughway. The operation was a debacle—badly organized, and poorly implemented. It resulted in Turkish forces sitting on higher ground with ill-fated Allied troops positioned like sitting ducks in the trenches below. The casualties were immense—a total of over 550,000 for both sides. Kitchener's reputation was another, although less dire, casualty.

During the war and under the government of Asquith, Lloyd George also served as minister of munitions. His methods were unconventional, surpassed only by his enormous energy. He recruited leaders from various business enterprises and persuasively induced organized labor to fall in line with his plans for war preparedness.

Lloyd George was scheduled to travel to Russia with Secretary of War Field Marshall Lord Kitchener on June 5, 1916. An unanticipated incident prevented him from boarding the H.M.S. *Hampsire,* which later struck a German mine west of the Orkneys. The cruiser settled to the bottom of the Atlantic within ten minutes of the explosion. The boatloads of survivors from the blast were drowned in the heavy seas. Among those lost was Lord Kitchener.

The death of the Secretary of War left a gaping hole in Asquith's government. While the prime minister assumed the responsibilities of the office, a permanent replacement was essential. Who would he choose to fill Lord Kitchener's shoes? Asquith penned a note to Lord Stamfordham, private secretary to King George V, which read:

> All this canvassing and wire-pulling about [Kitchener's] succession, while poor K's body is still tossing about in the North Sea, seems to me to be in the highest degree indecent.
>
> We can carry on here very well for a few days, and I am sure it would be a great mistake to be hurried into taking a precipitate decision.[130]

After much discussion and soul-searching, Lloyd George was appointed to fill Kitchener's vacancy in the War Office. The situation with the British military continued to decline even as the Germans marched into Romania. It was during this time that the new war secretary, Lloyd George, delivered what would come to be known as his "knockout blow" conversation with the United Press Association. He was adamant that there would be no negotiated peace:

> 'Britain has only begun to fight. The British Empire has invested thousands of its best lives to purchase future immunity for civilisation.

This investment is too great to be thrown away
.... The British are not disposed to stop because
of the squealing done by Germans, or done for
Germans by probably well-meaning, but mis-
guided, sympathisers and humanitarians ....
For two years the British soldier had a bad time.
No one knows so well as he what a bad time
.... He took his punishment. Even when beaten
like a dog, he was a game dog. When forced to
take refuge in a trench, when too badly used
up to carry the fight to his enemy, he hung on
without whining .... There is neither clock
nor calendar in the British Army today. Time is
the least vital factor. Only the result counts, not
the time consumed in achieving it .... There
is no disposition on our side to fix the hour of
ultimate victory after the first success. We have
no delusion that the war is nearing an end. We
have not the slightest doubt as to how it is to
end .... The fight must be to the finish, to the
knockout.[131]

By the close of the year, British troops were in a grave
situation. Robert Lloyd George indicated in his book, *David*

and Winston, that Churchill was the singular influence in Lloyd George's elevation to the role of prime minister when Asquith resigned on December 5, 1916. He had been a dynamic peace-time leader, but the energy required to guide Britain through the minefield that was World War I strained his commitment and perseverance.

David Lloyd George stepped into the role and took up the reins of government. At the age of fifty-four, he had reached the pinnacle of his career. One of his first moves as prime minister was to pare the unwieldy War Cabinet from twenty-three to five—a move that greatly reduced the amount of time it took to make decisions. His war strategies were successful on some fronts—alleviating the threat of a food shortage—and disastrous on others, chiefly his tactic to place the British army under the command of the French.

2

To many, it appeared Lloyd George had taken office as prime minister just in the nick of time. New policies regarding the war were crucial, resulting in a drive to attack the Ottoman Empire. The prime minister badly needed a win in his column, as well as an option for saving British lives on the Western Front. He began the deployment of troops stationed in Egypt; their purpose was to attack Palestine and move into Mesopotamia.

Under the command of Sir Archibald Murray, the Egyptian Expeditionary Force (EEF) of the British Royal Army struck out across the Sinai in December 1916. Following the coastline as Napoleon had in 1799, they took Al-Arish and Rafah with little opposition. From there the EEF moved up into southern Palestine.

In a letter to his brother, William Lloyd George that was penned in March 1917, David wrote of the incursion into Palestine:

> We are not far from Jerusalem and although it is not going to fall yet, I am looking forward to my Government achieving something which generations of the chivalry of Europe failed to attain.[132]

In Gaza, they found the Turks heavily entrenched. Murray hurled his troops at the line, but victory eluded them. Grave casualties drove them back, and Murray was faced with the same predicament that had beset Friedrich Kress von Kressenstein in 1915.[133] The English leader responded just as his German counterpart had before him: He replenished his troops and attacked the fortress at Gaza again in April 1917. The results were the same; Gaza sand soaked up the blood of Englishmen and Indians. The Turks had prepared by bringing in troops from the German Expeditionary Force, the Asienkorps.

Back in England, Prime Minister David Lloyd George was livid. He was a Protestant and passionate advocate of Zionism. He was captivated by the idea of returning the Jews to their homeland, and was very open about his biblical knowledge of the children of Israel. Lloyd George wrote: "Palestine, if recaptured, must be one and indivisible to renew its greatness as a living entity."[134] There is little question that Lloyd George's religious beliefs, and especially as a dispensationalist, had a great influence on the choices he made as prime minister. His ideology clearly impacted his political decisions regarding the Balfour Declaration in 1917.

Murray was relieved of command of the EEF and replaced by Field Marshall Edmund Allenby, 1st Viscount Allenby, a dogged and tenacious fighter nicknamed "The Bull." Before embarking for the Middle East, Allenby was summoned to No. 10 Downing Street, where Prime Minister Lloyd George made it abundantly clear that the British had no intention of suffering a third defeat in Palestine. Allenby was to marshal his strength, his wisdom, and his troops to present the British people with a Christmas present—Jerusalem.

Allenby arrived in Egypt in June 1917 and went directly to the front near Gaza. He quickly recognized that another frontal assault would be a suicide mission, and he set about devising a better plan. While he was working on this plan, unexpected news arrived: T. E. Lawrence, also known as Lawrence of Arabia, and a handful of Bedouins whose loyalty he had gained had managed to cross a nearly impassable desert to reach Aqaba by land. Aqaba's heavy guns faced the

Gulf waters, the only anticipated avenue of attack. Lawrence and his charges took the town by complete surprise and accomplished his goal. Lawrence planned to persuade the Turks that, not Aqaba, but Damascus was the target of the attackers. When a group of Arabs that included Lawrence moved against Aqaba as many as 300 Turks were viciously butchered, and an equal number were captured. Lawrence did not go unscathed; he suffered injuries when thrown from his camel.

The effect of the capture of Aqaba was more than valuable for Allenby. It served to protect his rear and right flank should he accomplish his plan—to break the Ottoman line at its eastern point, Beersheba. On October 31, the British fleet began to bombard Gaza relentlessly. At the same time, a British scout allowed himself to be spotted by Turkish sentries. In his flight, he purposely dropped a courier pouch. Inside, the sentries found what appeared to be secret British plans for an imminent and massive assault on Gaza, not unlike those employed by General Murray.

The Turks took the bait. To make ready for the attack, they moved a sizeable body of troops from Beersheba to Gaza to help man the trenches there. Only a small garrison was left at Beersheba. Meanwhile, a large complement of British troops moved to within easy striking distance of the town. They were guided by maps compiled four years earlier by surveyors Claude Conder and Horatio Kitchener, and by up-to-date intelligence reports from a network of Jewish spies living in Palestine. When the troops received the signal to attack, they swarmed Beersheba with lightning speed and accuracy. The Turkish garrison was stunned and quickly retreated to Gaza.

It was Allenby's moment to take Gaza. Fortified by naval support, aircraft for reconnaissance and support—a first for the EEF—and with tanks (their first deployment in the Holy Land), Allenby drew up his battle plan. Within nine days, Gaza had fallen.

Early in his days as minister of munitions Lloyd George had been greatly influenced by at least one Jewish man, Chaim Weizmann, who, during the war years, would be responsible for the manufacture of acetone, a much-needed ingredient for the manufacture of munitions. A chemist, Weizmann, had developed a method for making the vital chemical from chestnuts. When called to London to be honored for his service, Weizmann reacted with: "I require no honour for myself but I would like to ask something for my people."[135] It would be the beginning of a relationship between the chemist, Arthur Balfour, and the future prime minister, Lloyd George.

Weizmann had proven to be a lucid and convincing propagandist for the Zionist movement. Two newspaper editors had first introduced him to Lloyd George, Arthur James Balfour, Winston Churchill, and Lord Robert Cecil. With his commanding physical appearance and charming English, laced with a Russian accent, Weizmann adapted his arguments to each listener with unusual skill. With Britons and Americans he would use biblical language to awaken deep emotions. With Lloyd George, a Welshman, he emphasized Palestine's topography, which was much like that of Wales. With Balfour, who came from an Evangelical background, he explored Zionism; and with Lord Cecil, he spoke in terms of a new world organization. With other British leaders he stressed the extension of British imperial power inherent in the plan.

The Evangelical heritage of many of Weizmann's listeners worked in his favor. These men had read the Old Testament and were familiar with it to a degree unparalleled by their Catholic allies in France and Italy. To them, the children of Israel and the land of Canaan were to be venerated.

Prime Minister David Lloyd George will also be remembered for his inclination toward Zionist ideology, perhaps even more so than Arthur Balfour. Though it is said that he lost his faith at an early age, Lloyd George had an innate predisposition toward the ancient land of Israel. He freely admitted he was well-versed in the geography of the ancient Holy Land—more so than with his indigenous country of Wales.

From the time the Jews were thrust out of their homeland in Palestine, there has been an innate desire to return. It was this yearning that spurred the foundation by Theodor Herzl of the Zionist movement in 1896. When the first Zionist congress was held in Vienna, there seemed little hope that the Ottoman Turks would allow Jews access to Palestine. The result was that talk of establishing a new homeland turned to such locations as the Sinai Peninsula or Uganda. Herzl met with members of the Balfour government in 1903 to try to reach a workable solution for a Jewish settlement. In an attempt to find assistance, he contacted the law firm of Messrs. Lloyd George, Roberts & Co in London. The "Lloyd George" was, in fact, David, whose star in British government was in its ascendancy. He had, it seems, made quite a name for himself as a defender of human rights.

Herzl and his Zionist colleagues were but one group represented by Lloyd George and his associates, but it was the one faction that provided a wealth of information and knowledge about Zionists and Jews. Neither the young

Member of Parliament nor his cronies could know that Britain would play a significant role in the future of a tiny nation that would one day be labeled the State of Israel.

Imperialism may have been the clearest motivation in the call for the support of a Jewish homeland in Palestine, and it captured the imaginations of Lloyd George and Lord Balfour, who served under him. Both men were raised to be dedicated Christians and consistent church attendees, and they had a great familiarity with the Old Testament history of the Jewish people. The two men realized the historical and spiritual magnitude of the Jews returning to the Land promised by God to Abraham.

Years later, another U.S. president would echo Lloyd George while speaking at a meeting of *B'nai B'rith* (the global voice against anti-Semitism). Lyndon B. Johnson said, "The Bible stories are woven into my childhood memories as the gallant struggle of modern Jews to be free of persecution is woven into our souls."[136]

3

To hundreds of thousands of Protestants, including Lloyd George with his overwhelming compassion for the downtrodden, the real significance of what came to be known as the Balfour Declaration bolstered their belief that the Jewish people had a biblical destiny rooted in their ancient homeland in Palestine. Many felt their divine calling was to see this come to fruition. It was said that:

> The Balfour Declaration came, as it were, *ex cathedra* from on high . . . . it was not debated in either of the Houses of Parliament and like most foreign policy issues, was never approved by the British legislature . . . . A vigorous historical debate has raged for decades as to the

British cabinet's motivation in making this declaration . . . . Early explanations in the wake of the Great War emphasized the idealism of the British political elite and the religious sympathy among British Protestants for the idea of the restoration of the Jews.[137]

Another, more materialistic explanation for the Balfour Declaration offered a very dissimilar account. Leonard Stein offered this suggestion in his 1961 book *The Balfour Declaration*:

British propaganda efforts to win American- and Russian-Jewish support for the war effort, and the advantages such a Jewish homeland would . . . . [ensure British] strategic military control of the Near East.[138]

In November 1917, Lloyd spoke to a group in Paris, offering a rather provocative oration whereby he condemned so-called Allied "victories". His use of sarcasm was not appreciated by some Members of Parliament, and they let Lloyd George know of their displeasure. While he survived the uproar, the German offensive was fortuitously slowed on the Western Front by the daily introduction of 10,000 fresh American troops. The speed with which they were deployed was attributed to the use of British and French war materiel left behind, making it possible for the Americans to travel more lightly. The Germans were faced with dwindling reserves and a declining determination, a situation of which Lloyd George was determined to take advantage.

The following story is told by Col. R. Rawlinson, a young British army officer who worked in the War Office. It was indicative of Lloyd George's thirst for knowledge. Rawlinson and another young officer were sent to deliver secret documents to the home of David Lloyd George in December 1917. The two young men were cordially received, fed, and offered the customary cigar following dinner. The prime minister reviewed the documents while the men ate, and then seemingly ravenous for details from the front lines, "began to pepper the two soldiers with questions about the real conditions at the front, about rations, weapons, organization, leave, the spirit of the troops, the behavior of the enemy."[139]

On November 11, 1918, following an Allied rout of the weakened German army, an armistice was signed, and World War I ended. Lloyd George was forced to decide whether to continue the coalition he had formed during the war years or return to the party politics of a newly peaceful Britain. He chose the coalition method, which created a huge rift between the prime minister and the

Liberal Party, forcing him into an uneasy alliance with the Conservatives.

When called to Versailles at the end of the war, Lloyd George proved his prowess as a negotiator between French Prime Minister Georges Clemenceau, who had become prime minister in 1917, and U.S. President Woodrow Wilson. Lloyd George is credited with the creation of a more palatable treaty. (In recognition of his efforts at Versailles, the Order of Merit was presented to David by King George V in August 1919.) To the heads of state seated around the table at Versailles, the pro- and anti-Zionism factions were no more than a minor irritation. It was problematic to concentrate on Palestine and a future Jewish homeland when the fate of the entire world lay in their hands. There were, however, two groups in attendance that felt deeply about the Palestine issue: One group was comprised of Zionists; the other of Christian Arab missionaries who sought to stop the plan of the Zionists to establish a Jewish homeland on Palestine's soil.

In actuality, the peace agreement of World War I signaled a major change: the transition of Zionism from an imprecise and insular yearning to a universal political cause. It was contentious and alarming to many in Christian circles but welcomed by most of the principals. In April 1920, representatives of the Allied Powers and other world leaders gathered in Paris to begin to fulfill Balfour's vision and grant a mandate over Palestine to Britain. The wheels of what had begun as a dream for the likes of William Blackstone were set in motion.

In 1922, Prime Minister Lloyd George was driven from office by the opposition and would never hold another government position. He did serve as leader of the Liberals from 1926 to 1931, but the Labour Party had declined to the point that it had become the main opposition party to the Conservatives. Even in his retirement years, however, Lloyd George stirred a bit of controversy when, in 1936, he traveled to Berlin to meet with Adolf Hitler. Upon his return to England he wrote an article for the *Daily Express*, in which he gushed:

> I have now seen the famous German leader and also something of the great change he has effected. Whatever one may think of his methods—and they are certainly not those of a parliamentary country, there can be no doubt that he has achieved a marvelous transformation in the spirit of the people, in their attitude towards each other, and in their social and economic

outlook . . . . One man has accomplished this miracle. He is a born leader of men. A magnetic and dynamic personality with a single-minded purpose, a resolute will and a dauntless heart.[140]

Of course, by the time Hitler breached the Munich Agreement, Lloyd George was no longer a proponent of appeasement or of the German leader's tactics. In May of 1940, the British government met for what has become known as the Norway Debate. It was perhaps Lloyd George's finest hour as he eloquently called for the resignation of Prime Minister Neville Chamberlain. He saw Chamberlain as incompetent and ineffective and took the prime minister to task for it:

> Will anybody tell me that he is satisfied with what we have done about aero planes, tanks, guns, especially anti-aircraft guns? Is anyone here satisfied with the steps we took to train an Army to use them? Nobody is satisfied. The whole world knows that. And here we are in the worst strategic position in which this country has ever been placed.[141]

The seventy-seven-year-old orator summed up by saying:

The Prime Minister must remember that he has met this formidable foe of ours in peace and in war. He has always been worsted. He is not in a position to appeal on the ground of friendship. He has appealed for sacrifice. The nation is prepared for every sacrifice so long as it has leadership, so long as the Government show clearly what they are aiming at and so long as the nation is confident that those who are leading it are doing their best. I say solemnly that the Prime Minister should give an example of sacrifice, because there is nothing which can contribute more to victory in this war than that he should sacrifice the seals of office [or resign].[142]

The result of the debate was Chamberlain's removal as prime minister and Winston Churchill being named in his stead. Churchill offered Lloyd George a position in his War Cabinet, which the elder statesman refused. Two months before he died in 1945, at home in his beloved Wales, the title "Earl Lloyd-George of Dwyfor" was bestowed upon him.

David Lloyd George was articulate, charming, and persuasive. He had what some might call "second sight"—the ability to quickly discern the heart of complex problems and offer reasonable and responsible answers. He possessed a sincere dislike for those who maltreated the lowly, whether imprisoned by poverty or race. Conversely, he was enamored by the use of devious methods to achieve his goals, and he possessed a streak of callousness that limited friendships. He was accused of not giving enough thought to those appointed to office or selected for special honors.

It is said that in the latter years of his life, he became much more timid and given to hypochondria, but regularly attended the Castle Street Baptist Chapel in London. In 1944, as his life neared an end, Lloyd George went home to Wales. Ill health prevented him from taking his seat in the House of Lords, and he died at the age of 82 with his wife, Frances (whom he married after Margaret's death), and daughter Megan at his side.

Truthfully, however, he withdrew from politics when he was needed most—just before another devastating world war. When he might have been in the middle of the fray, he was sidelined by ill-health and forced to become a powerless onlooker. It was one of the tragedies of the war years, but his achievements while in office far outweighed the perceived failures in his later life.

In Israel, Lloyd George is memorialized in the village of *Ramat David* near Haifa. It is a farming community that bears the name of the British prime minister under whose auspices the Balfour Declaration was endorsed.

WALTER CLAY LOWDERMILK

The Holy Land can be reclaimed from the desolation of long neglect and wastage and provide farms, industry, and security for possibly five million Jewish refugees.

—WALTER CLAY LOWDERMILK

1

Most little boys like to play in the dirt, but when Walter Clay was born on July 1, 1888 to Henry Clay and Helen Vashti Lawrence Lowdermilk, his elated parents had no idea he would grow up to be a noted soil conservationist. Nor could they be aware that Walter would become a staunch Zionist who would have an agricultural impact on Israel, during the country's formative years.

Walter was born in Liberty, Randolph County, North Carolina, but his family didn't stay in the Piedmont Region long. Like the proverbial tumbleweed, Walter's parents moved first to Missouri, then Oklahoma, and finally trekked across the Desert Southwest to Arizona. After completing his secondary education, Walter became a student of

Park College Academy in Missouri, and then returned to Tucson to attend the University of Arizona. He was awarded a prestigious Rhodes scholarship at Oxford from which he received a B.A. and an M.A. degree.

The curriculum at the English university permitted Walter time during the summers to study forestry in Germany. It came when Herbert Hoover's Commission for Relief in Belgium challenged Lowdermilk and other young Americans in Europe to enhance their studies and volunteer for the program. The commission was established following the German invasion of Belgium in 1914. The small country was able to produce only about one-fourth of the food required for its citizens—most of which had suddenly been requisitioned by invading German troops. Starvation was looming if a source of food could not be found—and quickly.

A plan to get supplies into the country was developed by Millard Shaler, an expatriate living in Belgium. He contacted U.S. Ambassador Walter Hines Page to seek help from Herbert Hoover, then a mining engineer and financier living in London. (Hoover would become U.S. president in 1929.) Hoover enlisted a group of volunteers to help breach the British blockade and deliver the life-saving food. The Germans resented Hoover's interference by the Commission for Relief in Belgium (C.R.B.). Its relief ships contracted by Hoover were often sitting ducks for German submarines. This was despite agreements that had been put in place to safeguard the transports against attack by either the German or British navies.

Although clearly marked as C.R.B. vessels, not every ship survived the gauntlet and arrived safely in Belgium. The *Harpalyce* was torpedoed and fifteen sailors aboard were killed in April 1915. Despite the casualties, George Gay, a member of the commission, wrote that " . . . . the C.R.B. bought and shipped 11.4 billion pounds (5.7 million tons) of food to 9.5 million civilian victims of the war."[143] More than 11 million Belgium men, women, and children were fed because of the heroic efforts of those who joined hands and hearts with the C.R.B. One official with the British government called the effort, "a piratical state organized for benevolence."[144]

After returning to Oxford following his participation as a volunteer with the commission, Lowdermilk completed his tenure and went home to Arizona. He, then, began his career as a Forest Service employee in the Southwest until the United States sent troops to Europe. Walter was tapped as a timber acquisitions officer. An article from The Forest History Society explains:

When the United States entered the First World War in April 1917, one of the first requests from their French and British Allies was for regiments of trained lumbermen. Timber was in constant demand for almost every phase of military operations in Europe [especially because of the need for lumber in fortifying trenches], and limitations on trans-Atlantic shipping space meant that nearly the entire timber supply had to come from French forests. In order to maintain this supply, the forests would have to be carefully managed. The Allies agreed that American forestry units would work in France's forests, producing materials in accordance with the principles of French forestry. The U.S. Army, with assistance from the U.S. Forest Service, state foresters, and lumber trade associations, immediately began recruiting experienced foresters, loggers, and sawmill workers for these new regiments.

The 10th and 20th Engineers operated in various areas of France's forestlands, managing forest growth, felling and logging timber, and operating sawmills .... The wood was used for building roads and railroads, constructing barracks, erecting telephone poles, supporting trenches, and various other building and construction projects. The already highly experienced men making up the regiments were able to streamline the lumber manufacturing process almost immediately . . . . The forestry units would greatly exceed all expectations of production. The mills they operated produced over three times their rated capacity. [145]

After a successful stint in the Army, Lowdermilk returned to the U.S. Forest Service to conduct research in Montana. Although he was content with his work there, his life would change in 1922. While studying and working abroad, Walter had begun to correspond with a young Methodist missionary, Inez Marks, who had been stationed in China between 1916 and 1921. When she was furloughed home to Arizona the pen pals finally met, and marriage soon followed. The couple was sent to China where Walter again made his mark as a teacher at the American University in Nanking. He traveled the vast country helping the Chinese develop ways to halt soil erosion and combat famine. In his book, *Conquest of the Land Through 7,000*

Years, Lowdermilk wrote of the vital necessity of battling hunger:

> My experience with famines in China taught me that in the last reckoning all things are purchased with food. This is a hard saying; but the recent world-wide war shows up the terrific reach of this fateful and awful truth. Aggressor nations used the rationing of food to subjugate rebellious peoples of occupied countries. For even you and I will sell our liberty and more for food, when driven to this tragic choice. There is no substitute for food .... Food buys our division of labor that begets our civilization.[146]

Walter and Inez were forced to flee China when the Communist uprising began in March 1927. Back home in the U.S., Walter rejoined the Forest Service to continue his studies related to erosion while working toward his Ph.D. from the University Of California School Of Forestry at Berkley.

By 1933, Lowdermilk had been appointed to the short-lived Soil Erosion Service as assistant chief. It was a transitional post prior to the creation of the Soil Conservation Service, an agency that evolved into the Natural Resources

Conservation Service. Today, it is an arm of the U.S. Department of Agriculture.

The climatic, and climactic, event that came to be known as the Dust Bowl catastrophe in the U.S. hit South Dakota in 1933, and spread southward into the panhandles of Texas and Oklahoma by 1934. Nearby areas in New Mexico, Colorado, and Kansas were also affected by the drought with the blowing dust that sometimes reduced visibility to less than three feet. Because of agricultural development in the Plains, over-cultivation, and the lack of precipitation, the winds from storms sweeping through the area picked up massive amounts of topsoil and carried it eastward, sometimes as far as Boston and New York City. Pauline Winkler Grey wrote of the destruction in Kansas when "The Black Sunday" storm hit on April 14, 1935:

> It was as though the sky was divided into two opposite worlds. On the south there was blue sky, golden sunlight and tranquility; on the north, there was a menacing curtain of boiling black dust that appeared to reach a thousand or more feet into the air. It had the appearance of a mammoth waterfall in reverse—color as well as form. The apex of the cloud was plumed

and curling, seething and tumbling over itself from north to south and whipping trash, papers, sticks, and cardboard cartons before it. Even the birds were helpless in the turbulent onslaught and dipped and dived without benefit of wings as the wind propelled them. As the wall of dust and sand struck our house the sun was instantly blotted out completely. Gravel particles clattered against the windows and pounded down on the roof. The floor shook with the impact of the wind, and the rafters creaked threateningly. We stood in our living room in pitch blackness. We were stunned. Never had we been in such all-enveloping blackness before, such impenetrable gloom.[147]

As a result of the devastation on human life caused by the brutal dust storms, Lowdermilk was dispatched in 1938, first to Europe and then to the Middle East—Algeria, Tunisia, Tripoli, Egypt, Lebanon, Syria, Iraq, Trans-Jordan, and Palestine—to study how various peoples had made use of their land down through the generations.

2

As a dedicated Christian, Walter Lowdermilk was delighted to have the opportunity to visit Palestine, the historic land of the Bible. He would be given leeway to explore historic use of the land and develop methods of increasing the production of food. He would discover that his inspiration would come from Jews residing in the inner-cities of Europe who had reclaimed land for planting gardens.

Lowdermilk's invitation to study the use of irrigation to provide food for Palestine was not the first. As early as 1918, reports detailing the possibility of farming large portions of Palestine had been submitted to a committee consisting of Chaim Weizmann, Lord Rothschild, and Sir Alfred Mond. Other plans followed, but no sponsors of such a project could be found within the confines of the British government that oversaw the region. It was not until the proposal submitted by Walter Lowdermilk that the potential was revealed. As with other plans, it was subjected to the anti-Zionist prejudices that gripped other European nations. Far too often, propaganda won out over common sense in the need to feed the people of Palestine.

As Walter toured the countries of the Middle East, he rapidly acquired a vision for the fiscal transformation of Palestine. He proposed that the Jordan River Valley be developed, and that the rivers of the Upper Jordan be redirected into channels that could be used for irrigation of the surrounding lands. He also recommended a plan that would utilize waters diverted from the Mediterranean to provide power to the area. It was Lowdermilk's belief that under his plan as many as the 1.5 million people already in the region, as well as another four million Jews fleeing Europe could be accommodated in Palestine. His calculations were based on four dynamics:

- ✧ 3 million people had inhabited Palestine in Roman times;

- ✧ The climatic conditions had not changed since them;

- ✧ Jewish agricultural colonization had demonstrated that the restoration of the soil was possible;

- ✧ The climatic and geophysical conditions of the area were very similar to those of Southern California where the problems of soil erosion and irrigation had been most successfully tackled.[148]

Perhaps it was because of Walter's international recognition through the publication of various articles that his studies had gravitas. He was known to be a prominent authority on matters of the soil. In 1939, Lowdermilk wrote what he labeled, "The Eleventh Commandment." Delivered over the airwaves on Jerusalem Radio and dedicated to the Jews who had worked so hard as good stewards of the land, he said:

> Thou shalt inherit the holy earth as a faithful steward, conserving its resources and productivity from generation to generation. Thou shalt safeguard thy fields from soil erosion, thy living waters from drying up, thy forests from desolation, and protect thy hills from overgrazing by the herds, that thy descendants may

have abundance forever. If any shall fail in this stewardship of the land, thy fruitful fields shall become sterile stony ground or wasting gullies, and thy descendants shall decrease and live in poverty or perish from off the face of the earth.[149]

Lowdermilk had pondered what Moses might have thought of man's exploitation of the Promised Land God had given them. It had gone from being "a land flowing with milk and honey"[150] to a land of desolation. According to Rabbi Menachem Posner with Chabad.org:

Fruit trees grow in many different terrains, but their produce overflow with nectar only when the land is especially fertile, when the trees are particularly well-nourished.

Similarly, livestock survives in many habitats, but only overflow with milk when they are in particularly fertile pastures.

Thus, a "land flowing with milk and honey" is indicative and symptomatic of a greater good—the fertility of the Promised Land.[151]

Lowdermilk was certain that Moses might have added another commandment to those delivered by Jehovah—one that governed man's responsibility to care for the land he had been given.

Lowdermilk began his tour of the Arab-held lands in Palestine in shock and consternation. The land that had once been abundant and productive now looked much like Oklahoma during the Dust Bowl era: overtaken by sandy slopes and dry wadis. The agriculturist determined that some three inches of topsoil had been lost due to neglect. The Jews, on the other hand, had made great strides over a relatively short period of time. Lowdermilk thought they had confronted great adversities and used high standards of teamwork for conserving the soil. The Jews had exhibited an amazing penchant for the recovery of the abused lands he had witnessed on several continents.

Lowdermilk contended that just as the Tennessee Valley Authority (TVA) in the United States had utilized water to provide energy for industrial purposes and irrigation for farmers in the Southeast, the same concept could be used in Israel to make the desert bloom. This, in turn, would allow the land to support more displaced Jews in Palestine. He believed:

The Holy Land can be reclaimed from the desolation of long neglect and wastage and provide farms, industry, and security for possibly five million Jewish refugees from the persecutions and hatreds of Europe in addition to the 1,800,000 Arabs and Jews already in Palestine and Trans-Jordan.[152]

While not openly calling for a Jewish homeland in Palestine, Lowdermilk was sensitive to the plight of the exiled Jews worldwide. He opined:

> Some place must be found to reinstate the Jews long without a country among the peoples of the earth . . . . [the Jews] have already demonstrated the finest reclamation of old lands that I have seen on three continents [and] they have done this by the application of science, industry, and devotion to the problems of reclaiming lands, draining swamps, improving agriculture and livestock, and creating new industries . . . . [all done] against great odds with sacrificial devotion to the ideal of redeeming the Promised Land.[153]

Lowdermilk had long been deeply committed to the return of the Jews to their ancient homeland as outlined in Scripture. He was equally devoted to helping the Children of Israel revive the land in order to support its inhabitants. Upon his arrival in the country for the first time, he was overwhelmed with the history of his crossing. He wrote in *Palestine, Land of Promise*:

> In February, 1939, we, like the Children of Israel, left the land of Egypt before daylight...we crossed the southern part of the Land of Goshen, which Joseph had given to his brothers...we entered the Sinai Desert, where the Israelites and their flocks and herds had wandered for forty years.[154]

Walter was joined in his love for Zion by Inez, who had learned of Israel at the knee of her Methodist-minister father. Walter had dedicated his book on Palestine to his wife, his "comrade and inspiration."[155] One disconcerted British attaché opined that Inez saw herself as a modern version of an Old Testament prophet.

It could be that the British elite feared the reach of Zionism. It was considered to be a likely threat to their hold over the Middle East. Little did they know that a far greater threat—Adolf Hitler's "final solution"—was about to be unleashed upon the world. Nor did Lowdermilk know that he would be one of those riding the crest of the wave that would become the rebirth of the Nation of Israel.

When Walter arrived back in the States, he delivered his findings to Henry A. Wallace, Franklin D. Roosevelt's vice president during Roosevelt's third term in office. When Wallace reviewed the reports, he labeled Lowdermilk "the most complete Zionist . . . . anyone could ask for."[156]

3

Walter Lowdermilk was a prominent backer of the Zionist alliance both in his home country and in Britain during World War II and into the postwar years. He held membership in the American Palestine Committee, the aim of which was to raise support for the return of Jews to their homeland. He was also active in the Christian Council on Palestine. According to author Paul Merkley, Lowdermilk was "often in the company of other committed Christian supporters of Zionism in the United States such as the theologian Reinhold Niebuhr, the philosopher Carl Friedrich and Senator Owen Brewster."[157] Walter and Inez participated in Christian conferences throughout the U.S., appeared before the House and Senate, and spoke frequently to various Zionist organizations.

Walter's soil conservation programs were held in high regard and were swiftly embraced. He was invited to join the Palestine Survey Committee, an august group of men comprised of Dr. Nahum Goldmann (founder of the World Jewish Congress), Israel Sieff (prominent English business-man and Zionist), Emanuel Neumann (education director of the Zionist Organization of America—ZOA), and Morris Rothenberg (executive member of the ZOA.)

The Biltmore Conference, held in May 1942 in New York City, was attended by a number of members from various Zionist organizations. Members of the group called for the following:

. . . . the fulfillment of the original purpose of the Balfour Declaration and the Mandate which recognizing the historical connection of the Jewish people with Palestine' was to afford them the opportunity, as stated by President Wilson, to found there a Jewish Commonwealth. The Conference affirms its unalterable rejection of the White Paper of May 1939 and denies its moral or legal validity. The White Paper seeks to limit, and in fact to nullify Jewish rights to immigration and settlement in Palestine, and, as stated by Mr. Winston Churchill in the House of Commons in May 1939, constitutes 'a breach and repudiation of the Balfour Declaration'. The policy of the White Paper is cruel and indefensible in its denial of sanctuary to Jews fleeing from Nazi persecution; and at a time when Palestine has become a focal point in the war front of the United Nations, and Palestine Jewry must provide all available manpower for farm and factory and camp, it is in direct conflict with the interests of the allied war effort.[158]

On the basis of Lowdermilk's scientific soil studies and findings, several of the rabbis in attendance at the conference urged that Jews be allowed to immigrate to Palestine. Obviously, such pronouncements incurred the ire of Arab communities, both in the U.S. and in Palestine. Lowdermilks' proposals were misinterpreted as sanctioning forcibly removing Arabs from Palestine. Nothing could have been further from the truth; Walter wrote in *Palestine, Land of Promise* that the Arab inhabitants would "benefit greatly from the JVA [Jordan Valley Authority]. The increased Jewish immigration would provide them with new opportunities for investment and labour."[159]

Lowdermilk's book, though technical in content, was and still is, an infinitely enjoyable and fervent account of what life in Palestine could be with proper conservation measures. It pointed out in detail the great contrast between lands overseen by Jewish residents—land reclamation, flourishing farms, and the control of malaria—compared to those under Arab control.

After retiring from his stint with the Soil Conservation Service, Lowdermilk continued to aid the Israelis by employing some of the ideas he had set forth in his book *Palestine, Land of Promise*. Many Jewish agronomists preferred agriculture over food imports. Later, Israeli Minister of Development Mordecai Bentov (1955–1961) explained their attitude with the saying, "We don't need powdered milk; we need Lowdermilk."[160]

Lowdermilk has been described as "the world-renowned American expert on soil conservation that supported the development of the State of Israel, and guided and inspired this Department from its first days."[161] In 1976 Lowdermilk Forest was dedicated on the northern slope of Mount Tu'ran. When the ceremony was conducted, a Dr. Baum from the University of California delivered this reflection:

Future biographers of Dr. Lowdermilk will study in two places. One is the Bancroft Library where his papers are kept . . . . the other . . . . is the land of Israel, where his biography is written in the valleys, the hills, and the water.[162]

Journalist Rory Miller wrote of Lowdermilk:

For in providing such an attractive, considered, and passionate scientific argument for the creation of a Jewish state in the crucial decade following the introduction of the White Paper, Lowdermilk, perhaps more than any other elite opinion on both sides of the Atlantic his belief that "the movement for establishing a Jewish national home in Palestine is one of the most remarkable records of a people's struggle for national survival and self-expression".[163]

The noted agriculturist was honored when Technion University in Israel established the Lowdermilk Department of Agricultural Engineering. It stressed basic science as the foundation for the study of agriculture. Before students could move forward into that chosen field, they were required to take two years of chemistry, physics, biology, mathematics, and geology. In order to earn a four-year degree, a fifth year had to be devoted to a work-related venture. It is a fitting honor to a true visionary.

THEODOR HERZL

*If anyone thinks that Jews can steal into the land
of their fathers, he is deceiving either himself or
others. Nowhere is the coming of Jews so promptly
noted as in the historic home of the Jews, for the
very reason that it is the historic home.*[164]

—THEODOR HERZL

1

Although the discussion of modern Christian Zionism in any form would of necessity include men such as Arthur Balfour, William Hechler, and William Blackstone, it must then be quickly followed by Jewish Zionist Theodor Herzl. The works of these men in the arena of the restoration of the Jewish homeland are very closely intertwined. Theodor (Binyamin Ze'ev) Herzl was born in Budapest in 1860. His parents, Jeanette and Jakob, had dropped many of the accouterments of earlier times, dispensing with the more orthodox beliefs of the Jewish faith. They taught Theodor no Hebrew or Yiddish. It was all a consequence of the *Age of Enlightenment* that would allow Jews to be absorbed into European culture, to own property, and to move on an equal footing socially with others of that time and place. Theodor was reared as a "thoroughly emancipated, anti-traditional, secular, would-be German boy."[165] He regarded Judaism with "mocking cynicism"[166] and thought religion to be unsophisticated.

Theodor was the second child of a family that was Jewish in name only and who seldom observed any aspect of their religion. On his thirteenth birthday, Herzl's family held a confirmation for him rather than the traditional *bar mitzvah* normally celebrated for a young Jewish boy. He had an early interest in engineering but lacked the necessary prowess to pursue that study. He was remembered as a precocious and morose daydreamer.

Had Herzl received a traditional religious education he could have become a great rabbinical leader, but he would never have attended a secular high school or university. His language might then have been Yiddish only, instead of the four languages in which he was fluent—Hungarian, French, German, and English. Familiarity with the political thought and nationalism of Europe, knowledge of legal matters, awareness of the problems of economy, initiation into international diplomacy in all its intricacies—all would have been denied him.

Herzl was a man of striking appearance. He was handsome, with a regal bearing that made a lasting impression on all who came in contact with him. At the age of eighteen, following the death from typhus of his sister, Pauline, Theodor and his parents moved to Vienna. There he studied law, but did not practice it. Herzl soon joined *Albia,* a German nationalist student fraternity. During his involvement with the organization, he encountered the term "anti-Semitism," which had recently been coined by Wilhelm Marr, considered to be a "yellow journalist." Marr wrote that the Jewish race was attempting to enslave Germany. He was joined in his beliefs by German philosopher and economist Eugen Karl Dühring, author of *The Jewish Problem as a Problem of Race, Morals, and Culture.* Dühring's tome was well-known as an assault against Jewish cultural influence in society and repudiated any Jew's right to marry outside their race calling for their immediate removal from public office.

Herzl and other members of *Albia* attended a League of German Students rally intended as a memorial for noted composer Richard Wagner. Although the musician's works had been written long before the rise of the National Socialist, or Nazi, movement in Germany, he had enormous influence on the party's leader, Adolf Hitler. Wagner, in *Das Judenthum in der Musik,* penned in 1850, described Jewish music as taciturn, apathetic, trifling nonsense. In a later volume, *Deutsche Kunst und Deutsche Politik*, he wrote of the "harmful influence of Jewry on the morality of the nation."[167]

As Herzl listened to the artist being honored by the *Albia* delegate whose pro-German, anti-Semitic harangue was so excessive that the police were called to intervene, he determined to immediately submit his resignation. His dream of being accepted by the nobility of German authors was dashed.

During Theodor Herzl's days in Austria, he encountered Baroness Bertha von Suttner, the wife of Baron Arthur Gundaccar von Suttner. The baroness had been born in 1843 to Sophie von Koerner Kinsky, shortly after the death of her father, Count Franz Josef Kinsky. As a child under the guardianship of her father's best friend, Landgraf von Fürstenberg-Weitra, she wanted for little. However, after her guardian's death, the widow's portion allotted to Bertha's mother covered fewer of their needs.

The young Ms. Kinsky found herself in a most uncomfortable position. She was not aristocratic enough to please the upper echelon of society; therefore, she had to employ the skills she learned in the social circles in which her guardian traveled. Bertha was fluent in German, English, French, and Italian, and capitalized on her musical ability. She took on the job as governess to the four daughters of

Baron von Suttner, with whose family she had summered in Baden-Baden.

While attending to the education of the von Suttner daughters, Bertha fell in love with the youngest son of the household, Baron Arthur von Suttner. Bertha was seven years older than the young Baron, whose mother felt scandalized by the turn of events. With the realization that the family was less than pleased about the budding relationship, Bertha packed her bags and accepted a position in Paris as the secretary of Alfred Nobel (of Nobel prize fame.) As she prepared to leave the von Suttner household, Arthur knelt "before her and humbly kissed the hem of her gown, saying. 'Thy love has taught me to know a happiness which shall consecrate all my life. Farewell.'"[168]

Bertha soon received a telegram from her beloved Arthur in Vienna. She gathered up her belongings and quickly made her way back in response to his avowal that he could not live without her. The two young people eloped and then settled in the Caucasus (present-day Georgia). After nine years and some softening by Arthur's parents, they returned to Austria, where Bertha became a noted writer.

In Vienna, the Baron and Baroness formed a friendship with Theodor Herzl. Bertha thought him to be charming and striking, clever and congenial. She said of him:

He also sparkled with wit. And that head of his—like an Assyrian king's! He ought to have been really king of the new Zion, whose awakener he was, and which might perhaps already exist if he had not died so prematurely.[169]

Just two years after their first meeting, Herzl enticed Bertha to use her relationship with Czar Nicholas II to secure an audience with the Russian ruler. In a letter to Suttner, Herzl stressed four areas where Jewish influence might be of assistance to the Czar: 1) offensive and hurtful pogroms would disappear from the landscape; 2) young Jews with a zeal for revolution would be assuaged; 3) those organizations touting revolution would be weakened; and, 4) the number of Jews in Russia would be diminished by relocation. Even though Bertha pled Herzl's case not once but twice, an audience with Nicholas II was denied.

Although they felt differently about the other's pet projects—*Abwehrverein* (anti-Semitism) for von Suttner and Zionism for Herzl—each developed a great respect and admiration for the other. It was her friendship with Herzl that turned the Baroness from a German liberal into a philo-Zionist.

Herzl's personal life was filled with difficulty. In 1889, he married Julie Naschauer, who was susceptible to erratic mental behavior. The couple followed no Jewish customs, instead celebrating Christmas with all its accoutrements. Herzl failed to follow one of the major practices of the Jewish faith; his son was not circumcised. His wife had no interest in her husband's Zionist involvement although it had been her dowry that subsidized Herzl's activities. Subsequently, they had three children who were predisposed to the same mental issues as their mother.

After a brief attempt at a legal career in Vienna and Salzburg, Herzl devoted himself to journalism and literature. He became a Paris correspondent for *Neue Freie Presse*. While working as a journalist during the Dreyfus Affair, and when he heard the crowds taunting the unfortunate French Jewish army captain with shouts of "death to the Jews," it became his own critical moment of recognition—nothing would be acceptable except a Jewish state, a sovereign nation. The Dreyfus trial was Herzl's initial experience with naked anti-Semitism and it convinced him that only in their homeland could the Jews find safety from this evil, ugly thing. For the first time in his life, he began to attend Jewish religious services.

The headlong rush into adopting a stance of anti-Semitism was exacerbated by the mayor of Vienna, Karl Lueger, a coarse rabble rouser. It was said of the city leader:

> Lueger was extremely popular with the lower middle classes, largely because of his folksy and vulgar speeches uniting popular economic and religious antisemitic prejudices. He succeeded in forging a party which channeled social discontent, depicting capitalism and Marxism alike as products of the Jewish mind and fusing these new themes with the centuries-old hatred of the Jews stemming from Church doctrine . . . . His administration pursued discriminatory practices against Jews, mainly through not employing them in the city services and limiting their numbers in high school and the university.[170]

As Herzl watched the howling mobs running rampant through the streets of Vienna, he correctly concluded that what had come to be known as anti-Semitism would one day be lawful in other European countries.

2

To understand the drastic transformation of Theodor Herzl, one must be well-informed of the facts concerning the Dreyfus Affair. Alfred Dreyfus, a Jew and a little-known soldier in the French army, came under suspicion of spying when, in 1894, papers were found in the trashcan of a German officer. It appeared that Captain Dreyfus was guilty of providing military information to Germany. He was arrested, dragged before a tribunal, stripped of his rank, convicted, and summarily dispatched to Devil's Island—a notorious, disease-ridden prison on the coast of French Guiana in South America. The liberal newspapers of the day crucified the former captain, labeling his actions "Jewish treachery." Meanwhile, Dreyfus' friends worked diligently to disprove the charges against him. He was eventually pardoned and allowed to return to France, but only after ten, horror-filled years on Devil's Island. Although his commission in the French army was restored and he was promoted to the rank of major, he never recovered from his years of isolation, deprivation, and disease.

While covering the trial of Alfred Dreyfus, the young Jewish reporter was forever changed. Theodor Herzl rejected his family's earlier religious ideas regarding emancipation and assimilation and came to believe that the Jews needed to remove themselves from Europe and create their own state. He finally came to grips with his Jewish heritage and embraced the ideology he had not been taught as a child. Herzl soon became well-known as a fighter for a homeland for his people. As Christian apologist Reinhold Niebuhr later wrote:

> The majority group expects to devour the minority group by way of assimilation. This is a painless death, but it is death nevertheless.[171]

More and more, Herzl turned to his writing, penning such stage plays as *The New Ghetto*. In 1895, he wrote his seminal treatise *Der Judenstaat* (*The Jewish State*). The release of the book immediately identified Herzl with political Zionism. In the book, he outlined the reasons

Jews should return to their historic homeland, then called Palestine. He wrote:

> The Jewish question persists wherever Jews live in appreciable numbers. Wherever it does not exist, it is brought in together with Jewish immigrants. We are naturally drawn into those places where we are not persecuted, and our appearance there gives rise to persecution. This is the case, and will inevitably be so, everywhere, even in highly civilized countries—see, for instance, France—so long as the Jewish question is not solved on the political level. The unfortunate Jews are now carrying the seeds of anti-Semitism into England; they have already introduced it into America.[172]

Among Herzl's friends was French writer Alphonse Daudet, to whom he went for advice two years before writing his first novel, *Old-New Land*:

> "When I told him I wanted to write a book for and about the Jews, he asked: 'A novel?' 'No,' I ventured, preferably a man's book.'" (Novels were, at that time, deemed to be women's books.)

To which Daudet replied: "A novel reaches farther. Remember *Uncle Tom's Cabin*?"[173]

As Palestine was controlled by the Ottoman Empire in 1896, Herzl attempted an audience with Turkey's Sultan Abdul Hamid II to present his solution for a Jewish state. He failed to gain a meeting, and was warned that should he attempt to move forward, he might fall prey to the sultan's scimitar of jail. Herzl did not ignore the threat. (The two would meet five years later, but the Sultan refused Herzl's offers to help merge the Ottoman foreign debt for a charter allowing Zionists an entrée to Palestine.) Later that year, Herzl returned to London to address a mass rally of thousands, most of them recent Eastern European Jewish immigrants in that city's East End. He was received with great esteem and was granted the mandate of leadership for Zionism. From that point, the movement grew rapidly.

The Jewish State proffered a blueprint for the reestablishment of a state in the Holy Land. Herzl was fortunate to have as a Christian friend, William Hechler, with ties to the Kaiser's family. Like the children of Israel, who wandered in the Sinai with no map or GPS, Herzl could not see the path before him; but the Jewish people would see the end result of that journey.

In 1897, at great personal expense, Herzl founded *Die Velt* (*The World*), a Zionist weekly, in Vienna. He often selected what he deemed interesting articles and forwarded them to Kaiser Wilhelm. In the same year, Herzl undertook the First Zionist Congress in Basle, Switzerland. He rented the Basle Municipal Casino, "hung a white flag with two blue stripes and a six-sided star over the entrance . . . . so the delegates would associate it with the old Jewish flag. Blue and white were the colors of the Hebrew prayer shawl."[174] Before the beginning of the first session, Herzl attended services at a synagogue in deference to the religious Jews whose support he needed. He managed to deliver a blessing in halting Hebrew, and later opined that he had perspired more in that few minutes than when giving a speech.

When Herzl spoke at the First Zionist Congress, he openly acknowledged the role his Christian associates had played in the formation of the Zionist organization. Author Montefiore wrote: "There was nothing new about Zionism—even the word had already been coined in 1890—but Herzl gave political expression and organization to a very ancient sentiment."[175]

Herzl was certain that at Basle he had founded the Jewish state. He wrote in his diary, "If I said this out loud today, I would be greeted by universal laughter. Perhaps in five years and certainly in fifty, everyone will know it."[176] He was elected president (a position he held until his death). When he mounted the podium to give his first address to the group, the audience proclaimed, "Yehi ha-melech," (long live the King) a reference to King David. In 1898 Herzl began a series of diplomatic moves intended to build support for a Jewish nation. In October of that year, he traveled to Jerusalem for his first visit to that city. Several years later, he would address the British Royal Commission on Alien Immigration. That secured an introduction to Joseph Chamberlain, Colonial Secretary of State. With contacts made through the British government, Herzl secured a charter with the Egyptian government for a settlement of the Jews in the Sinai Peninsula adjoining Southern Palestine. The move would fail, however, when it was decided by negotiators that the Nile River could not support a Jewish colony in the region.

Herzl also attempted to gain support for a Jewish homeland from Pope Pius X, but Catholic hierarchy explained that so long as the Jews denied the divinity of Christ, the Church would certainly not make a declaration in favor of any such Jewish state.

3

In Theodor Herzl's diaries, which were an important written chronicle of his life and attempts to secure a Jewish State, he wrote often of Philipp Michael de Newlinski. It was Newlinski he credited with contacting certain important Turkish leaders on his behalf. According to Dr. Saul Rafael Landau, who supposedly had an impressive list of political contacts among the Poles, Herzl was advised to meet with Newlinski. Landau wrote, "During his diplomatic service in Constantinople, [Newlinski] had made friends with the Turkish Sultan Abdul Hamid and that he was the Sultan's confidential agent in Vienna."[177] This would be an important liaison, as the Turks would have to be persuaded, coaxed, and cajoled onboard with any plan for a Jewish homeland in Palestine.

Newlinski was the son of an old patrician Polish family and a law student at the University of St. Petersburg. He forfeited his law career for journalism and published periodicals in both St. Petersburg and Moscow. It was this endeavor that caught the attention of Count Julius Andrassy, the man who would become Russian foreign minister. Because of Newlinski's extraordinary comprehension of Russia's course of action in the Balkans, Andrassy enlisted him to serve as his advisor. This position led Newlinski to develop personal ties with the Turks and was the reason Landau recommended him to Herzl.

On May 7, 1896, Herzl and Newlinski met for the first time. Herzl records in his diary that his new friend had, indeed, read *The Jewish State* and had talked with the Sultan about its contents. Newlinski revealed to Herzl that the Sultan would "under no condition give away Jerusalem where the Mosque of Omar is situated, which must remain in Muslim hands."[178]

After several months of correspondence between the two men, Herzl ultimately persuaded Newlinski to accompany him on a trip to Constantinople to meet with the Sultan and introduce him to the Zionist cause. The two men boarded the Orient Express and set off for their appointment with the Ottoman ruler. The trip was an eye-opener for both of the travelers, as they stopped at various cities along the way. Herzl was able to experience firsthand Newlinski's charismatic interaction with members of the Bulgarian government and with the Bulgarian Church. At the same time, Newlinski witnessed Herzl's popularity among Bulgarian Jews who had traveled to Sofia to zealously welcome the Jewish leader to their country.

En route to Constantinople, Newlinski was of invaluable assistance in discussions on how to advise and prepare Herzl for interaction with the Sultan, especially with regard to talks of how to revitalize Turkey's financial assets. Upon arrival in June 1895, Newlinski went to work establishing discussions between Herzl and high-ranking Turks, all the while setting the stage to fulfill Herzl's desire to meet personally with the Sultan. He also ensured that Herzl would meet Grand Vizier Rifat Pasha, as well as officials from the Russian Embassy who held great sway with the Turks.

When told by Newlinski of Turkey's financial difficulties, Herzl, still working to obtain another audience with Wilhelm II, tried to raise millions in funds to aid the sultan with the country's financial calamity. None of his friends and associates were willing to invest in the project designed to increase support for a Jewish homeland in Palestine.

Newlinski, in an audience with the Sultan prior to an introduction of Herzl, was advised that the Sultan was "in no position to give away a single foot of territory, since it did not belong to him but to his people. 'Let the Jews save their billions.' The Sultan continued, 'When my empire is partitioned, they may get Palestine for nothing. But they will only be able to divide up our corpse. I am not ready to submit to vivisection.' On the subject of a constitutional government, the Sultan replied sarcastically that a constitution had not saved Poland from being partitioned."[179]

Herzl might have been deterred from his mission after hearing the Sultan's discourse, but it only spurred him to redouble his efforts to seek an audience with the ruler. Herzl's eyes were firmly fixed on the vision of an established, ordered homeland for the Jewish people. Newlinski responded by introducing Herzl to Agostino Danusso, an agent who, for a predetermined sum, would secure information—some secret—from the Sultan's court. He also acted as a scribe to translate Zionist papers into Turkish and dispense them to targeted individuals.

Herzl wrote of his friend Newlinski:

> "His character appeals to me more and more,
> as I get to know him better. If he had enough

money, he would be one of the most magnificent grand Seigneurs and might have become one of the world's leading diplomats." Herzl went on to characterize his friend as "obliging but proud, crafty and yet sincere, too, and his unmistakable gentlemanly qualities are detrimental to his reputation . . . . He is the most interesting figure I have had to deal with since I have carried on the Jewish cause."[180]

Newlinski's labors were unflagging as he worked to successfully bring the Sultan and Herzl together. While one diplomat urged Herzl to enlist the Czar of Russia in his Zionist cause, Newlinski was persuaded that Palestine would be given to the Jews by the Turks; it was only a matter of time.

The Sultan summoned Newlinski on June 26. During the audience, he asked Newlinski if Herzl and his Zionist friends might consider an exchange rather than the outright purchase of Palestine as a Jewish homeland. He asked if the Jews were adamant about Palestine or if they might consider an alternative. Newlinski responded, "Palestine is the cradle of the Jewish people and that is where they wish to return."[181] Though unable to secure an introduction for Herzl, Newlinski persuaded the Sultan to bestow upon

Herzl the Order of Medjidie (a military and knightly order)[182] and was, at least, able to tell the Sultan about Herzl's plans for a Jewish state.

Herzl and Newlinski departed Constantinople three days later, unsuccessful but unbowed. Herzl's friend and companion next suggested an introduction to his friend Otto von Bismarck. They would attempt to enlist him in helping to sway the Sultan toward a Jewish homeland in Palestine. (*The Newbery House Magazine* published an article in 1893 that revealed Bismarck had formulated his own plan for a homeland for the Jews.)

So indebted was Herzl to Newlinski that he recorded in his diary, "I promised Newlinski my lifelong friendship. If we should ever obtain Palestine with his help, we will repay him by presenting him with a beautiful estate in Galicia."[183]

Newlinski continued to work behind the scenes to promote Herzl's plan for a Jewish homeland. In August 1896, he wrote Herzl and asked him to submit a detailed proposal to be presented to the Sultan. The plan called for a twenty-million-pound sterling loan to Turkey. In return, the Sultan was to agree to Jewish emigration to Palestine without Turkish limitations. The proposal stagnated until January 1897, when Newlinski was informed that the Turks openly resented Herzl. They blamed him for an anti-Turkish article published in the *Neue Freie Presse* (a Viennese newspaper).[184]

In a rebuttal published in Newlinski's paper, *Correspondance de l'Est,* he wrote:

> The sole aim of Zionism is to bring about the new reunion of the Jews as a people, a race and a nation in the ancient land of their forefathers, under the rule, the sovereignty and the protection of Turkey, by means of successive settlements of Jewish laborers, land owners and industrialists . . . . There is nothing else in that program and it merits nothing but approval and encouragement . . . . the Jews who were being persecuted everywhere, want nothing but hospitality and protection in Turkey . . . . Politically Turkey had nothing to fear, and Jewish immigration could only benefit her. On the whole, Jews show gratitude to nations which help them.[185]

Newlinski continued his fight to help Herzl until his death on April 1, 1899. He took one last trip to Turkey to again try to attain approval from the Sultan for a homeland in Palestine. While in Sofia, Bulgaria, he suffered a heart attack and died. Ironically, in the telegram to Herzl announcing Newlinski's death was also a notice that the Sultan would have permitted him an audience on April 4, 1899. It would be two long years after Newlinski's death before Herzl was finally permitted to meet with the Sultan.

Newlinski embraced the aspects of secret diplomacy—the back-room deals, exploiting the written media, the wheeling and dealing—that brought him a certain fulfillment and opened doors for him in the courts and political circles of the day. Through his great efforts, he secured his place in the annals of Zionism.

Although firmly setting the course of action for the Jews' return to their homeland, Herzl would not live to see the culmination of his work. He died of cardiac sclerosis on July 3, 1904. A day before his death, he instructed the Reverend William H. Hechler to , "Greet Palestine for me. I gave my heart's blood for my people."[186] Herzl had indeed given himself for and to his people without holding back, spending his great gifts with prodigal generosity until his death at the age of forty-four. Though this champion of a Jewish homeland was gone, his work continued through men such as Chaim Weizmann and others.

Theodor (Binyamin Ze-ev) Herzl was buried in Vienna. In 1949, after the rebirth of the Jewish homeland, his remains were exhumed and moved to Jerusalem. He was reburied on Mount Herzl overlooking the spreading, modern city he never saw, but which owes its existence in no small measure to his labors.

Tragically, none of Herzl's children survived him. Eldest daughter Pauline died a drug addict in a hospital in France in 1930. His son Hans, who had departed from Judaism and became involved in several Christian churches, committed suicide when he learned of his sister, Pauline's, untimely death. The youngest Herzl daughter, Trude, was murdered at Theresiendstadt, a Nazi concentration camp, along with her husband. Their son Stephen Theodore Newmann (later Norman) committed suicide on November 10, 1946. After hearing of his parents' deaths, he flung himself from the Massachusetts Avenue Bridge in Washington, D.C. He was only twenty-seven years old. Mercifully, Herzl did not live to endure the sorrow of the deaths of his children and only grandchild, who was also his only descendant to embrace Zionism.

DAVID BEN-GURION

If a land has a soul, Jerusalem is the
soul of the Land of Israel.[187]

—DAVID BEN GURION

1

As David Lloyd George was making his mark in British political circles, another young David was finding his way to Palestine from the *shtetl* (village) of Płońsk, Poland, then part of the Russian Empire. His name was David Grün (Green). He was born in 1886 to attorney Avigdor Grün and his wife, Scheindel. His mother died when David was eleven. (In 2003, a copy of his birth certificate was unearthed in Poland. It indicated that David's mother had borne twin sons; one died shortly after birth.)

In his memoirs, David wrote of his life in Płońsk:

> I personally never suffered anti-Semitic persecution. Płońsk was remarkably free of it . . .

Nevertheless, and I think this very significant, it was Płońsk that sent the highest proportion of Jews to Eretz Israel [Land of Israel] from any town in Poland of comparable size. We emigrated not for negative reasons of escape but for the positive purpose of rebuilding a homeland . . . Life in Płońsk was peaceful enough. There were three main communities: Russians, Jews and Poles. . . . The number of Jews and Poles in the city were roughly equal, about five thousand each. The Jews, however, formed a compact, centralized group occupying the innermost districts whilst the Poles were more scattered, living in outlying areas and shading off into the peasantry. Consequently, when a gang of Jewish boys met a Polish gang the latter would almost inevitably represent a single suburb and thus be poorer in fighting potential than the Jews who even if their numbers were initially fewer could quickly call on reinforcements from the entire quarter. Far from being afraid of them, they were rather afraid of us. In general, however, relations were amicable, though distant."[188]

David received his education in a Hebrew school founded by his father, who was a passionate Zionist. Avigdor was a leader in the *Hovevei Zion*—Lovers of Zion—organization. It was not surprising, then, that at a young age David became the recognized leader of *"Ezra"*, a movement whose young adherents advocated the study of Hebrew and emigration to Palestine.

By the time he was eighteen in 1904, David found himself in the streets of Warsaw, hungry and struggling to earn enough to buy food. Even with minimal education, he worked as a teacher and strove to further his education despite governmental limitations on Jews attending Russian schools. While studying at the University of Warsaw, David joined *Poalei Zion*, the Social-Democratic Jewish Workers' Party.

When news reached him that his champion, Theodor Herzl, had died, David was overcome with grief. He explained his sadness to a friend:

> Only once in a thousand years is a man of miracles such as this born. Like the expanse of the sea is . . . . our loss. [He called Herzl] the great fighter and hero who . . . . awoke a people dwelling in tombs from the slumber of death.[189]

Eighteen months later, Grün would set out upon his journey to Palestine, where he would adopt the name David Ben-Gurion, eventually assume the mantle of Herzl, and help bring about the birth of his hero's dream—a homeland for the Jewish people.

When David arrived in Palestine, then under the control of the Ottoman Empire, he joined forces with agricultural workers to establish communes, which ultimately became the kibbutzim (collective farms). To his thinking, there was only one way to truly follow Zionism: take control of the Land by employing Jewish labor. David also became involved in pro-independence and socialist activities. By the start of World War I, he must have been on every list of people most likely to be a disruptive influence. He and Yitzhak Ben-Zvi (instrumental in forming the Jewish defense group *Hashomer* and Israel's second president after its rebirth) were soon apprehended and deported to Egypt by the Ottoman rulers.

Unwelcome and ousted from Palestine, Ben-Gurion traveled to New York City to plead the Zionist cause to Jews in the United States. While there, he met and married Paula Monbesz, who was also involved with the *Poalei Zion* organization. The couple had three children: Amos, and two daughters, Geula Ben-Eliezer and Renana Leshem.

David and Ben-Zvi returned to Palestine in 1918 as members of the Jewish Legion in the British Royal Fusiliers, brainchild of Russian Zionist Ze'ev Vladimir Jabotinsky. The two men had left Ottoman-controlled Palestine only to return to a land under the jurisdiction of the British.

Back in the Holy Land and still believing it would be Jewish labor that would provide the bedrock foundation for a new state, Ben-Gurion dove right into local politics. He established trade unions, specifically the General Federation of Labour or *Histradut*. As its representative, David attended World Zionist Organization and Jewish Agency meetings. In 1935, he was elected chair of both groups.

David crusaded unstintingly for Zionist ideas and ideals both in the United States and in Europe, as he also worked tirelessly to develop military strength in Palestine. At the onset of the Second World War, he actively encouraged Palestinian Jews to enlist in the Allied cause. At the same time, he was busy organizing an underground railroad to liberate Jews from the Nazis and help them escape to Palestine. Following the end of the war, as resistance against British rule became the focus, Ben-Gurion strongly denounced right-wing extremists who resorted to terrorism to make their case.

David Ben-Gurion, and men of similar beliefs, stood toe-to-toe against both the British who executed the mandate in Palestine and with the Arab inhabitants fighting the creation of a Jewish state. By the grace and hand of God, Ben-Gurion and his supporters prevailed. On May 14, 1948, the British withdrew from Palestine.

Soon thereafter, David Ben-Gurion stepped to the microphone and boldly declared the rebirth of a Jewish homeland. History records that:

> The ceremony was held in the Tel Aviv Museum (today known as Independence Hall) but was not widely publicised as it was feared that the British Authorities might attempt to prevent it or that the Arab armies might invade earlier than expected. An invitation was sent out by messenger on the morning of 14 May telling recipients to arrive at 15:30 [8:30 AM EST] (and to keep the event a secret. The event started at 16:00 (a time chosen so as not to breach the sabbath) and was broadcast live as the first transmission of the new radio station Kol Yisrael.[190]

The name of the new nation had not been decided—would it be Israel? Would it be Judaea? One thing was almost certain—full-scale war would erupt immediately, as had been promised by the Arab nations surrounding the tiny state. Of course, there were those who were convinced that the only way out was to turn the entire area over to the United Nations as its caretaker. Clark Clifford, political advisor to FDR and then to Truman, was much opposed to that move, which he felt would see the demise of a Jewish homeland before it had come to life.

Clifford had prepared a possible announcement for Truman to deliver shortly after the stroke of midnight. At their usual meeting days before the event was to take place, Truman outlined what he wanted the White House counsel to do in order to convince Secretary of Defense George Marshall to endorse the idea of a Jewish state:

> You know how I feel. I want you to present it just as though you were making an argument before the Supreme Court of the United States. Consider it carefully, Clark, organize it logically. I want you to be as persuasive as you possibly can be.[191]

All of the players on Truman's team—Marshall, Undersecretary of State Robert A. Lovett, political adviser David Niles, Clifford, and various aides—came together late in the afternoon on May 12. Dominant in the room where they met was the famous sign on the president's desk: THE BUCK STOPS HERE. As the men filed into the Oval Office, a mere two days separated them from the rebirth of the still-unnamed state. The surface calm in the room belied the underlying tension.

The meeting began with an overview of the situation and the Jews' confidence that things would go smoothly in the transition. George Marshall assured everyone present that he had given the Zionists notice not to expect assistance from the United States, even in light of the possibility of increased hostility. The secretary of state was angry because it was said that he had dispatched someone with a message to David Ben-Gurion—a statement he implacably denied. Additionally Marshall stated he had no idea who Ben-Gurion was. (He was, of course, the head of the Jewish Agency, and the projected first prime minister of the new state.)

Next in the rotation of speakers was Clifford, who presented his points succinctly. It was his last point that would fuel the fire of Marshall's intransigence. Clifford said:

> Mr. President, I strongly urge you to give prompt recognition to the Jewish state immediately after the termination of the British

Mandate on May 14. This would have the distinct value of restoring the president's firm position in support of the partition of Palestine. Such a move should be taken quickly, before the Soviet Union or any other nation recognizes the Jewish state. [He concluded:] I fully understand and agree that vital national interests are involved. In an area as unstable as the Middle East, where there is not now and never has been any tradition of democratic government, it is important for the long-range security of our country, and indeed the world, that a nation committed to the democratic system be established there, one on which we can rely. The new Jewish state can be such a place. We should strengthen it in its infancy by prompt recognition.[192]

When Marshall indignantly objected not only to the content of his statement but to Clifford's presence at the meeting, Truman laconically replied, "Well, General, he's here because I asked him to be here."[193]

The debate raged on as first Marshall and then Lovett joined the attack against recognition. Marshall was so incensed that he actually threatened Truman during the discourse. He wanted the president to be assured that should he side with Clifford (which he had already), the vote of the secretary of state would go to his opponent in the next election.[194]

Truman ended the meeting with the issue still unresolved between him, Marshall, and Lovett. Not only did Marshall record the entire discussion in the official record of the meeting, it has been said that from that time forward, he refused to even speak the name of Clark Clifford.

2

May 14, 1948, in the U.S. capital dawned unusually warm and humid. The anticipation in government halls was palpable: Would the president recognize a Jewish state or would he acquiesce to his secretary of state and postpone any acknowledgement? Unlike today's "instant news instantly" mindset, the transmission of information took a bit longer. What was going on in Jerusalem? How high was the anticipation there? How great was the threat of annihilation?

In the White House, Clifford was still attempting to sway Marshall and Lovett to the side of recognition. He approached Lovett with the question that if the secretary of state refused to support Truman on the matter, would he at least not openly defy him? After much vacillation, the general finally agreed to do nothing, neither positive nor negative. He would simply make no comment.

Clifford also contacted Eliahu Epstein, head of the Jewish Agency, and requested his assistance:

> Mr. Epstein, we would like you to send an official letter to President Truman before twelve o'clock today formally requesting the United States to recognize the new Jewish state. I would also request that you send a copy of the letter directly to Secretary Marshall.[195]

Working with several advisors, Epstein had drafted a succinct missive that reached the White House by noon on the fourteenth. His request as an agent of the Provisional Government of Israel read as follows:

> I have the honor to notify you that the State of Israel has been proclaimed as an independent republic within frontiers approved by the General Assembly of the United Nations in its Resolution of November 29, 1947, and that a provisional government has been charged to assume the rights and duties of government for preserving law and order within the boundaries

. . . . The Act of Independence will become effective at one minute after six o'clock on the evening of 14 May 1948, Washington time . . . . I have been authorized by the provisional government of the new state to tender this message and to express the hope that your government will recognize and will welcome Israel into the community of nations.[196]

In the original document, Epstein had referred to the new state simply as "Jewish state." As the letter was being delivered to Clifford by aide Harry Zinder, Epstein was advised by shortwave radio that the official name of the newly-established state would be "Israel." He immediately dispatched a second aide to overtake Zinder, strike the phrase "Jewish state," and insert "Israel" into the document.

At 6:11 that evening, White House Press Secretary Charlie Ross read the following statement dated May 14, 1948, approved and signed by President Harry Truman:

This government has been informed that a Jewish state has been proclaimed in Palestine, and recognition has been requested by the [provisional] government thereof. The United States

recognized the provisional government as the
de facto authority of the new [State of Israel].[197]

Just as Epstein's document had the added word "Israel" so had Truman's document. The United States of America, in the year of its 172nd anniversary, was the first foreign nation to recognize the sovereign State of Israel; the USSR followed three days later. The president's pro-Zionist advisors bore the brunt of criticism for Truman's actions; however, it was the feisty, fedora-wearing Missourian who made the final decision. Although Truman was the first foreign head of state to acknowledge the new nation, other heads of state soon took up the gauntlet to ensure that Israel would survive.

When Israel issued its declaration of statehood, Ben-Gurion assumed the offices of prime minister and defense minister. He demanded that the various armed factions be merged into one fighting force—the Israel Defense Force (IDF). He masterminded the creation of many of the burgeoning state's institutions and various internal projects to aid development (i.e., Operation Magic Carpet to airlift Jews from unfriendly Arab countries, the founding of new towns and cities, and a national waterworks along with other infrastructure projects). He continued to encourage pioneering and farming in the remote areas of the land.

Ben-Gurion achieved Herzl's dream, his passion for a Jewish state, and was then entrusted with its guardianship. The newly acknowledged State of Israel was all that Herzl had imagined. As Yoram Hazony, author, philosopher, and political theorist, wrote:

> Ben-Gurion found himself overseer of a state that was neither neutral nor multinational as Judah Magnes, Martin Buber, Lessing Rosenwald or the ever-present U.S. State Department had hoped to see formed. It was, instead, in the most precise way conceivable the state about which Herzl had written in *The Jewish State*—a place where non-Jewish residents were welcomed "to participate in the up-building of the state on the basis of full and equal citizenship," but one whose significance, single-mindedness, and function would nevertheless result in "the right of the Jewish people to be masters of their own fate . . . . in their own sovereign state."[198]

When Ben-Gurion stepped to the podium at 4:00 pm on that warm Friday afternoon in May, he carefully read the statement that would declare Israel's sovereignty. The following day, May 15, Egypt launched its military aircraft toward Tel Aviv in retaliation. It was Shabbat, and there was no official response until Saturday at the conclusion of the holy day. As the prime minister again delivered a news bulletin to his awaiting audience, he announced that an Egyptian warplane had been shot down, its pilot imprisoned, and the aircraft added to the Israeli Air Force. He also reported that the United States had been the first nation to recognize Israel's independence.

During his initial term as prime minister, Ben-Gurion established what were known as "nationality laws." This was likely the most important step toward fusing Israel into the cohesive state it has become. Simply stated, it meant that all immigrating Jews were immediately registered as Jewish nationals. The Star of David was chosen for its flag, the state seal exhibited the image of a *menorah*, and the Jewish anthem was "Hatikvah"—The Hope. All official holidays were centered on the Jewish calendar, and Shabbat was declared to begin at sundown on Friday and end at sundown on Saturday. Ben-Gurion urged the Ministry of Education to establish schools that would educate non-practicing Jews in the religious ways of life, which included wearing the prayer shawl and *tefillin* (phylacteries) when in prayer and observing bar and bat mitzvahs, among other customs. Additionally, it has been said that Ben-Gurion kept a Bible in his office and attended Bible studies twice each week.

Ben-Gurion left political life in 1953 and returned to his first love, *Kibbutz Sde Boker* in the Negev, but was called back into service in 1955 as minister of defense and then again to the office of prime minister following the two-year term of Moshe Sharett. The changes were spurred by what came to be known as the "Lavon Affair," which affected not only Sharett but also Ben-Gurion's eventual second term as prime minister.

The Affair was so named because Sharett's Minister of Defense Pinhas Lavon was charged with overseeing a rogue intelligence operation that was designed to inflict damage to U.S. and British interests in Egypt. On what seemed like a merry-go-round of events, Lavon was first found guilty of the charges, then absolved, then forced to resign his post. Reportedly the political ranks at the Ministry of Defense believed that Benjamin Givly, military intelligence chief and the prime minister's protégé, had formed a spy ring. The purpose of what came to be known as "Operation Susannah" was to cause disruption between the regime of Gamal Abdul Nasser and the West, or to in effect turn Israel's allies against her avowed enemies. Its overall aim was to convince the British not to withdraw from the Suez Canal Zone, which was deemed necessary to maintain a peaceful climate in the region.

One of the recruited spy cells was charged with placing homemade bombs on the shelves of libraries in Alexandria and Cairo, and another group set off a firebomb in an Alexandria post office. A theater owned by a British company was also targeted with an explosive device. It was fortunate that the acid and nitroglycerin devices did little damage and resulted in no injuries or deaths.

Perhaps appropriate for a plan infused with deception, the operation was calamitous for Israel, as one of the infiltrators turned informant and was later exposed as a double agent for the Egyptian government. The plan was made even more provocative with the use of Egyptian Jews as the moles. The Israelis charged that Nasser's regime staged the ensuing trial only for show. Two of the saboteurs were condemned to death by hanging. The Egyptian court, on the other hand, spared the majority of the participating infiltrators the death penalty. After serving part of their sentences, the Jewish partisans involved were eventually deported from Egypt to Israel. Sharett never quite escaped the political disgrace caused by the Lavon Affair. He wrote that Lavon had "incessantly advocated acts of lunacy, inculcating the army command with the diabolical notion of igniting the Middle East, fomenting disputes, bloody assassinations, attacks on objectives and assets of the powers, desperate and suicidal acts."[199]

Lavon met with Prime Minister Moshe Sharett and disavowed any knowledge of Operation Susannah. Givly proclaimed the minister of defense a liar and an inquiry was set in motion. The board of inquiry assigned to the case was unable to uncover irrefutable evidence that Lavon had actually sanctioned the mission. Lavon then tried to implicate Chief of Staff Moshe Dayan and sought to bring charges of insubordination and criminal negligence against Defense Ministry Secretary General Shimon Peres. When Lavon was forced to resign, Sharett convinced Ben-Gurion to return to the post of minister of defense. Soon thereafter, the prime minister resigned and Ben-Gurion once again assumed that office.

Ben-Gurion was soon to learn that Lavon had not gone "gently into that good night,"[200] as some had hoped he might. In 1960, new evidence was uncovered contending that the approval for Operation Susannah had been falsified, and Lavon requested a new investigation. A tribunal headed by Supreme Court Justice Chaim Cohen was appointed to investigate the matter, and as a result Lavon was cleared of the charges. Ben-Gurion apparently felt he could not accept the ruling without questioning the integrity of the Israeli military, and refused to clear Lavon's name. The prime minister declared that only a full judicial inquiry would be acceptable. A second committee was appointed and spent two months reviewing the Lavon Affair. It too reached the same conclusion: that Lavon was innocent of the charges. So strongly did Ben-Gurion believe justice had not been served, that on January 31, 1961, he submitted his resignation.

Only after Lavon was forced to resign his post as head of *Histadrut* (the country's organization of trade unions) was a mollified Ben-Gurion persuaded to withdraw his resignation and form a new government. Forced to stand for general election and barely able to put together a new coalition, Ben-Gurion never fully recovered from the acrimonious conclusion in what he deemed to be the bogus end of the Lavon Affair.

3

I n 1963, Ben-Gurion again abruptly resigned as prime
minister. There appeared to be little respect for the
man who had fought so long to see Zion returned to his
people. Two years after his departure, Shlomo Avineri, a
young political science professor at the Hebrew University,
wrote of Ben-Gurion:

> The specter of David Ben-Gurion, erstwhile
> national leader and secular Messiah . . . . now
> wandering in the political wilderness with a
> small band of followers . . . . Is he doomed to
> oil-age failure . . . . or is it a cold-blooded maneu-
> ver, calculated to bring about major changes

in Israeli society? . . . . However one evaluates
Ben-Gurion's contribution in 1948 . . . . no man
is indispensable in the long run. Government
[is] running smoothly.[201]

Many think the untimely end to Ben-Gurion's leadership
was directly related to the demands from John F. Kennedy's
administration that inspectors not only be allowed access to
a construction site near Dimona, but that if the site proved
to be a nuclear facility, it should be closed. This collision
course had been fixed during the last days of the Eisenhower
administration, as rumors surfaced that a top-secret struc-
ture had begun to rise in the middle of the Negev. It was
touted by the Israelis as a textile plant, from which visitors
were barred. Spy photos of the locale were emblazoned
across the front page of the *New York Times*.

The November U.S. election in 1960 ushered Senator
John F. Kennedy into the White House. During his 1,036
days in office, Kennedy made several decisions in favor of the
Jewish people. In 1961, he met in New York City with David
Ben-Gurion. In their meeting, Ben-Gurion shared with the
president, "We are the remnant of a people struggling for its
last hold of its existence. Israel is our last stop."[202] Throwing
tradition to the wind, Kennedy decided to sell surface-to-air

Hawk missiles to the Israelis to help defend against Arab attacks. The U.S. president was the first to do so, and in acquiescing to Ben-Gurion's request, defied the powerful and mostly anti-Semitic State Department and Pentagon. Then he tripled Israel's financial assistance from the United States.

The president seemed to understand what so many in the State Department refused to acknowledge then, and even today: That tension between Israel and her Arab neighbors was much more than a proliferation of arms. In his book *John F. Kennedy and Israel*, Herbert Druks wrote:

> The Arab leaders used Israel as their scapegoat and a means to gather popular support from their people. They claimed that all their troubles came from the fact that Israel existed. Instead of improving the life of their people in such countries as Egypt, Syria, Jordan, Lebanon, Arabia, Iraq, the Sudan and Libya they bought weapons with which to dominate and control other countries and to control their own people.
>
> For Israel it was a basic question of survival and not a desire to dominate or rule the world.

It was not a question of an arms race. Israel needed weapons in order to protect itself from such countries as Egypt, Syria and Iraq that sought its annihilation.[203]

Shortly after Kennedy's inauguration, the dispute over Dimona—had reached a fever pitch. Unlike another Democrat, Jimmy Carter, Kennedy was not fundamentally antagonistic; rather, he had a unique compassion for the Jewish people. Kennedy was pressed by his advisers—who presumed that Israel had no choice but to comply—to push for access to Dimona. In their zeal, Prime Minister Ben-Gurion was denied entry to the White House; instead, he and the president met at the Waldorf Astoria in New York City. Their talks were centered on the site in the Negev.

At that time, pre-1967, Israel was much more dependent on the backing of Jews abroad. Ben-Gurion recognized that sanctions and restrictions against donations from Jews in the United States would be devastating to the still-struggling country. For two years, the prime minister danced around U.S. demands.

Having reached the end of his tether, Kennedy wrote to Ben-Gurion on May 18, 1963. In his letter he warned that with further restrictions on U.S. inspectors, Israel would be cut off and completely isolated. This was apparently the straw that broke the prime minister's resolve; he tendered his resignation.

Levi Eshkol assumed the role of prime minister after Ben-Gurion's departure. Less than ten days after his induction, he too received a letter from President Kennedy, warning that the U.S. commitment to the Jewish state "could be seriously jeopardized."[204] Following John Kennedy's assassination, Eshkol took the same road—through the Lyndon Johnson and Richard Nixon administrations—as had his predecessor. The two countries finally settled comfortably into a "don't ask, don't tell" arrangement that has continued for more than forty years.

David Ben-Gurion remained an active force in the Knesset until he again retired completely from politics in 1970. He returned to *Sde Boker* where he lived until he suffered a brain hemorrhage and died on December 1, 1973. Officially noting the event, sirens sounded across the mountains and plains of Israel, and flags were lowered to half-staff, as the former prime minister lay in state in the courtyard of the Knesset. Following his funeral, Ben-Gurion's body was flown by helicopter to *Sde Boker*, where he was laid to rest beside his wife, Paula.

Today, Israel's international airport in Tel Aviv bears his name, as do Ben-Gurion University of the Negev in Beersheba, and numerous streets, avenues, and schools throughout the Holy Land. He is considered one of the founders and even, by many, the father of the State of Israel.

LORD ANTHONY ASHLEY-COOPER,

7ᵀᴴ EARL OF SHAFTESBURY

Let us not delay to send out the best agents . . .
to search the length and breadth of Palestine to survey
the land, and if possible to go over every corner of it,
drain it, measure it, and, if you will, prepare it
for the return of its ancient possessors
for I must believe that the time cannot be far off
before that great event will come to pass.

—LORD SHAFTESBURY

1

The Jewish people have always had their champions, even in the darkest of times—men and women from paupers to princes, and from laborers to lords. One such advocate was Anthony Ashley-Cooper, seventh Earl of Shaftesbury, a statesman, benefactor, and humanitarian. Born April 28, 1801 at Grosvenor Square in London, he was the eldest son of the Earl and his wife Anne Spencer-Churchill, daughter of the Duke of Marlborough. (Biographer Georgina Battiscombe wrote that Anthony referred to his mother as "a fiend" likely because she was said to have been "neglectful of her children."[205])

The family moved to their home in Dorsetshire after the elder Cooper ascended to the title of sixth Earl. Young Ashley-Cooper was sent away at the age of seven to a particularly disgusting school, Manor House (Chiswick), of which he later said, "The place was bad, wicked, filthy; and the treatment was starvation and cruelty."[206] According to his biographer, "He cried, when at home, at the thought of going back to school, and . . . . he cried, when at school, at the thought of going back to his home."[207] Following his sojourn at the hated academy, Ashley-Cooper was schooled at Harrow and then at Christ Church in Oxford. In 1841, he became a Doctor of Civil Law.

Shaftesbury's faith was not handed down to him from his parents, who were by all accounts bereft of affection for their children; he was introduced to the Bible and its evangelical teachings by Maria Millis, the family's housekeeper. She modeled Christ's love for him, and he owed his penchant for benevolent works to her. Author Geoffrey Best wrote, "What did touch him was the reality, and the homely practicality, of the love which her Christianity made her feel towards the unhappy child. She told him Bible stories, she taught him a prayer."[208] Through this mentor, Anthony was given the compass that would point him toward truth. She taught him to see God as kind, loving, and generous; the diametrical opposite of his exacting and self-absorbed father.

Of Shaftesbury, journalist Kevin Charles Belmonte wrote:

The driving force of all this social activity was his faith. Some of the more important guiding principles expressed in his writings include:

By everything true, everything holy, you are your brother's keeper.

Creed and color, latitude and longitude, make no difference in the essential nature of man.

Social reforms, so necessary, so indispensable, require as much of God's grace as a change of heart.

What is morally right can never be politically wrong, and what is morally wrong can never be politically right.

No man can persist from the beginning of his life to the end of it in a course of generosity, [or] in a course of virtue unless he is drawing from the fountain of our Lord himself.[209]

At one point during his life, Ashley-Cooper commented to his friend Edwin Hodder:

My religious views are not very popular but they are the views that have sustained and comforted me all through my life. I think a man's religion, if it is worth anything, should enter into every sphere of life, and rule his conduct in every relation. I have always been—and, please God, always shall be, an Evangelical.[210]

After completing his schooling in 1822, the young aristocrat found himself with no place to hang his hat. His father had forbidden him residence at the family homes at St. Giles and Grosvenor Square. Lord Ashley was reduced to depending on the indulgence of his friends. In 1823, he departed England for what was termed a "Grand Tour," an acceptable diversion for young men of that day.

Lord Shaftesbury joined parliament in 1826. Both tall and handsome, he cut a graceful swath among his friends and acquaintances. When called upon, he was articulate, forceful and precise although, by most accounts, not a silver-tongued orator. He married Emily, the daughter of Earl and Lady Cowper. After the death of her husband, Emily's mother married Lord Palmerston; a union that would prove to be a political boon to the young Earl. Shaftesbury and Emily produced ten children—six boys and four girls.

Being much more interested in philanthropic endeavors than political ventures, Shaftesbury joined a committee to investigate the treatment of the mentally ill. He personally visited the asylums that dotted the countryside and always left the facilities distressed over the lack of proper care for the inmates. He introduced a bill to amend the law concerning their treatment. Shaftesbury continued to work for reform of the so-called Lunacy Acts in order to lessen the severity and cruelty with which those thought to be insane were treated. As a Member of Parliament (MP), it was one of his first forays into philanthropy—one that he would espouse until his death.

Shaftesbury then began to instigate a change in the laws that governed factory and mill workers. It seemed a thankless task as, time after time, the bills he proposed to limit the number of hours the workers were on the job had been so undermined by other MPs that they were of little use. One of his speeches to the assembly left a deep impression with his description of those who had been sent to hospital due to job injuries. It was not until he left that august body in 1847 that changes were finally authorized. He continued to labor to bring new industry workers under the umbrella of the law. Shaftesbury wanted every man, woman, and child in Great Britain to be protected.

2

Even while laboring to aid factory and mill workers, the plight of those struggling in the nation's mines captured Ashley-Cooper's attention. He was appalled to learn that women and children struggled under the most exhausting and humiliating conditions imaginable. MPs Sir Lesley Stephen & Sir Sidney Lee wrote of Shaftesbury's report to parliament regarding the conditions under which many worked:

> Many women were found to be working in dismal underground situations, in such a way as tended to degrade them to the level of brutes. Children, sometimes not over four or five years of age, were found toiling in the dark, in some

cases so long as eighteen hours a day, dragged from bed at four in the morning, and so utterly wearied out that instruction, either on week days or Sundays, was utterly out of the question. Often they were attached by chain and girdle to trucks which they had to drag on all-fours through the workings to the shaft . . . .

The opposition were struck dumb by these revelations. An act was passed in 1842 under Ashley's care abolishing the system of apprenticeship, which had led to fearful abuses, and excluding women and boys under thirteen from employment underground.[211]

Shaftesbury assisted in forming unions to aid mill workers and delved deeply into the reformation of "ragged" schools for underprivileged children. They were so-called because the schools were free for destitute children. Students were taught reading, writing, some arithmetic, and the Bible. London's Field Lane was one such school visited by writer Charles Dickens:

I found my first Ragged School in an obscure place . . . . pitifully struggling for life under every disadvantage. It had no means; it derived no power or protection from being recognized by any authority; it attracted within its walls a fluctuating swarm of faces—young in years, but youthful in nothing else—that scowled Hope out of countenance. It was held in a low-roofed den, in a sickening atmosphere, in the midst of taint and dirt and pestilence; with all the deadly sins let loose, howling and shrieking at the doors. Zeal did not supply the place of method and training; the teachers knew little of their office; the pupils, with an evil sharpness, found them out, got the better of them, derided them, made blasphemous answers to Scriptural questions, sang, fought, danced, robbed each other—seemed possessed by legions of devils. The place was stormed and carried, over and over again; the lights were blown out, the books strewn in the gutters, the female scholars carried off triumphantly to their old wickedness. With no strength in it but its purpose the school stood it all out and made its way.[212]

Shaftesbury said in later life that if the ragged schools failed, he would not die of natural causes, but rather of a broken heart. One of his greatest loves was for the children of his homeland, and therefore his greatest efforts were expended toward providing for them at every level—and especially the lowest and the most destitute.

Shaftesbury also provided information to Lord Palmerston which was the basis for new laws that regulated the guardianship and reformation of juvenile offenders. The Refuge and Reformatory Union founded 589 residential homes that oversaw more than fifty thousand children. Ashley-Cooper's reformations extended to the homes of the less fortunate, but began with those on his estate. Each worker was furnished with a domicile on one-quarter acre of land. Each was equipped with the most modern appliances available, and for which the tenants paid only one shilling per week.

Building sites began to spring up around the country to offer better accommodations for the men and women whose labors undergirded Great Britain. Nor did Shaftesbury's efforts end there; he worked diligently to improve sanitary conditions, especially following the cholera outbreak of 1849. His efforts on disease control were such that Florence Nightingale, the noted nurse and social reformer, proclaimed they ultimately saved the British army during the Crimean War. It was Shaftesbury himself who said:

To love the public, to study universal good, and to promote the interest of the whole world, as far as lies within our power, is the height of goodness, and makes that temper which we call divine.[213]

3

While pursuing reformation for the poor, the Earl was introduced to several different religious organizations that provided assistance. The missionaries with whom he worked gave him an enlightening tour of the lodging houses in towns and cities. Charles Dickens accurately and graphically described the squalor in his novel *Bleak House*:

> It is a black, dilapidated street, avoided by all decent people, where the crazy houses were seized upon, when their decay was far advanced, by some bold vagrants who after establishing their own possession took to letting them out in lodgings. Now, these tumbling tenements

contain, by night, a swarm of misery. As on the ruined human wretch vermin parasites appear, so these ruined shelters have bred a crowd of foul existence that crawls in and out of gaps in walls and boards; and coils itself to sleep, in maggot numbers, where the rain drips in; and comes and goes, fetching and carrying fever and sowing more evil in its every footprint.... [214]

Those "lodging houses" provided a roof—for a fee—to as many as could be crammed together at night. Men, women, and children slept head-to-foot, side-by-side, without an inch to spare in between unwashed bodies. Unfortunately, no one was spared the debauchery that occurred in such a setting. Unable to legislate change to the existing establishments of the day, Shaftesbury set about to provide new and better future accommodations.

Not only did Shaftesbury's missionary associations ignite his attention to social reform, it also sparked his interest in the Bible, missions, and religious meetings. He aligned himself with the Young Men's Christian Association (YMCA), as well as the Church Missionary Society, and was president of the British and Foreign Bible Society for a number of years. His parliamentary honors and posts included commissioner of the board of control and lord of the admiralty.

From these associations would spring his desire to aid the Jewish people in their quest for a homeland. Shaftesbury was equally influenced by John Darby, who was described by writer Stephen Sizer as "the most influential figure in the development of . . . . Christian Zionism."[215] Sizer's assertion was made on the basis of Darby having for sixty years expounded upon his beliefs regarding dispensationalism on the European continent, in Great Britain, and in America. The result was the conversion of a number of significant Evangelical leaders, including William Blackstone, and Henry Moorhouse, a British theologian who introduced evangelist D. L. Moody to Darby's teachings.

Darby had broken free from the mindset of medieval Christians, who had embraced replacement theology as a basic tenet. As stated earlier, replacement theology rejects the concept that the promises God made to Israel are for this present hour; that instead, they were cancelled at Calvary. As a result, these promises fell to the Church, which, it was postulated, had replaced Israel. The belief that the Jews were cursed and condemned because of their refusal to believe in Jesus Christ as the Messiah permeated the medieval Church. Both Jewish and Christian Zionists came to believe that this teaching was at least partially accountable for the long and horrific history of anti-Semitism in Europe.

Darby emerged on the scene of British Zionism as one who challenged the liberal tendency toward interpretation of the Bible. His insightful delineation of the apocalyptic portions of Scripture had a significant and lasting impact on world mores. His teaching reached a zenith while it was said that the sun never set on the British Empire, thus making it easier to influence many worldwide. Though Darby was not political per se, he counted many prominent men as followers.

Darby basically taught it would not be the Church that brought blessings on mankind but a restored Jewish state in Palestine—the homeland of God's Chosen People. Furthermore, teaching that the Church did not replace Israel in God's plan; rather, that the Jewish people would return to Zion and seize their rightful inheritance.[216] Lord Shaftesbury was one of Darby's most significant allies. It was fortuitous that his place among the peerage commanded the respect of a number of influential politicians, among them his father-in-law, British Foreign Secretary Lord Palmerston. It was Palmerston who wrote in a letter to the British ambassador at Constantinople (known today as Istanbul):

There exists at the present time among the Jews dispersed over Europe, a strong notion that the time is approaching for their nation to return to Palestine.... It would be of manifest importance to the Sultan to encourage the Jews to return and to settle in Palestine because the wealth which they would bring with them would increase the resources of the Sultan's dominions; and the Jewish people, if returning under the sanction and protection and at the invitation of the Sultan, would be a check on any future evil designs of [Governor of Egypt] Mehmet Ali or his successors.... I have to instruct Your Excellency strongly to recommend to hold out every just encouragement to the Jews of Europe to return to Palestine.[217]

Shaftesbury was transformed into an untiring activist for Darby's dispensationalist teachings, and became an unabashed advocate of Christian Zionism. Writer Barbara Tuchman named him "The most influential non-political figure, excepting Darwin, of the Victorian age."[218]

This was true both in his personal and political life. He became an unstinting advocate through public intercourse via speeches, writings, and lobbying efforts. According to one author:

> He did more than anyone before him to translate Christian Zionist themes into a political initiative. In addition to influencing British colonial perceptions of the Near East, Shaftesbury also predisposed the next generation of British conservative politicians favorably toward the World Zionist movement, which led eventually to British support of the Jewish State.[219]

Edwin Hodder wrote with grandiose reverence of Lord Shaftesbury's later years, "As the outward man began to perish, the inward man was renewed day by day, and though the suppleness, strength and activity of the old body began to fail, the well-exercised soul grew stronger."[220] Ashley-Cooper attempted to perform his duties in Parliament, but by July 1885 found that his health was greatly taxed by those demands. His last act before his death was to visit the Home Secretary and then the House of Lords on behalf of children caught up in child prostitution. Though ill, his outrage knew no bounds as he addressed the group for more than a half-hour. On July 25, Shaftesbury traveled to Folkestone in hopes that he would be revived by the sea air. It soon became obvious that he was so ill he could not be moved to his beloved home. Friends and family rallied around him, and in his waning hours, Shaftesbury spoke to them of his profound faith and comfort in Christ. He died on October 1, 1885.

Although Shaftesbury had requested a simple burial service at St. Giles, it was not to be. Those for whom he had labored all his political life were determined to honor him at Westminster Abbey. The streets leading to the cathedral were lined with the poor—factory workers, chimney sweeps, flower-sellers, mill workers—each bedecked with some scrap of something black. It was a show of respect for the man who tirelessly fought to lessen the miserable circumstances under which they struggled.

AFTERWORD

Christian Zionism preceded modern Jewish Zionism,
and I think enabled it . . . . Today, Christians
by the thousands, by the tens of thousands, the
hundreds of thousands, by the millions, by the tens
of millions — today they have heard this call, and
they stand with Israel. I salute you, the people of
Israel salute you, the Jewish people salute you.

—PRIME MINISTER BENJAMIN NETANYAHU

Prime Minister Benjamin Netanyahu's statement regarding the effects of today's Christian Zionists is an affirmation of the men and women who helped return Jews to their homeland. The truth is that the vast majority of Zionists in the world today are Christians who love the land of Israel and her people, and are united because of their belief in Scripture. The prime minister's words have been echoed by many. American author Lawrence J. Epstein has said that few realize "how much Christians have contributed to the Zionist movement and to the nation of Israel."[221]

In support of the prime minister's hypothesis, there is story upon story of Christian Zionists who have been employed as instruments to aid the Jewish people in fulfilling God's covenant-promise to Abraham. Zionists—both Christian and Jew—are men and women who simply believe the Bible in regard to the covenant God made with Abraham some four thousand years ago. Through the reading of the Scriptures, they have been persuaded to support a Jewish homeland in Palestine. Some have given their lives, still more have invested their time and funds to help God's Chosen People return, rebuild, and restore the Holy Land, while others have prayed and interceded for the Jewish people.

Since that momentous announcement by David Ben-Gurion on May 14, 1948, Israel has had to fight for her very life—not once but multiple times. Joining the Jewish people in the trenches were sympathetic gentiles from around the world. With each succeeding battle for existence, new organizations—many of them established by Christian Zionists—have been formed to stand with the children of Israel in their battle to survive.

By the late twentieth century, Evangelicals had been infused with ever-growing numbers of those God-fearing people who bless Israel in daily prayer and intercession as well as proffering monetary support. Members of today's Christian Zionist organizations have great respect for the Jewish people and for Judaism. They believe that it is the very foundation upon which Christianity is based—after all, Jesus was a Jew who kept the entire Mosaic Law.

Evangelicals are not engaged in terrorist attacks against their enemies; they are not intent upon doing God's work on Earth *for* Him. They are, instead, advocates for the State of Israel; they are defenders of God's Word and His Chosen People. Many evangelical groups support programs that provide food, clothing, housing, and more for Jews who have returned to Israel, especially those from Russia. They employ whatever political clout has been amassed in order to stand in strong support of Israel. With over sixty million-plus Christian Zionists in the world, their presence remains a force with which to be reckoned.

Those who support the Jewish people have expended billions of dollars in assistance through orphanages, provided medical supplies, and sponsored social assistance programs for Israel's poor and needy. Information is dispensed through conferences in support of Israel, through promoting better understanding between Christians and Jews, by denouncing anti-Semitism and through prayer. Various groups have sponsored marches through Jerusalem in support of the nation and the right of the Jewish people to live in Israel. Many have aided Jews from Russia and other countries to immigrate to Israel.

In 2002, I founded the Jerusalem Prayer Team (JPT), which has been at the forefront of these efforts to provide assistance to the Jewish people. JPT has raised funds and invested millions of humanitarian dollars in Israel by providing food for the hungry, warm hats and coats for thousands of elderly Jews, basic necessities for Russian Jewish refugees, backpacks for school children, medical equipment for terror victims, and the preparation of a bomb shelter/community center in Jerusalem to be used as a safe place during terrorist strikes. It contains a kitchen, television sets, telephones, and much more. The Jerusalem Prayer Team is also helping to fund bomb shelters near schools for children to seek safety during attacks.

The stated purpose of the Jerusalem Prayer Team: To guard, defend, and protect the Jewish people and *Eretz Yisrael* until she is secure; to see Christians and Jews standing together to find better understanding of each other.

In 2012, I traveled to Jerusalem to seek a location for a Christian Zionism Museum in the Holy City. Through the museum, the accounts of Christians who played a crucial role in helping to promote, defend, support, and establish the modern State of Israel is told, as are the stories of those men and women who fulfilled the moral duty to rescue Jewish people from the Holocaust. The museum provides interactive displays, areas for research, and a bond between those Christian Zionists who have aided Israel through the years with the Jewish people. The vision of the Jerusalem Prayer Team is to have a place where their achievements are shared with thousands of visitors yearly. The attractive building housing the museum sits in the heart of Jerusalem at 20 Yosef Rivlin Street, a prominent location overlooking Independence Park and within walking distance to the Old City.

For decades, sympathetic gentiles from around the world have joined Jewish people in the trenches. With each succeeding battle for existence, new Christian Zionists have sprung up to stand with the Children of Israel in their battle to survive. These are the men and women the new Museum of Christian Zionism spotlights—those who have staunchly supported the Jewish people before, during, and after the formation of the State of Israel.

Today my heart is overflowing with gratitude to God as the dream He placed in my spirit more than thirty years ago—a dream I first shared with Prime Minister Menachem Begin—has become a reality. When the contract for the purchase of the building that houses the Jerusalem World Center—within walking distance of the Temple Mount in Jerusalem—was signed, I was reminded once again that every promise from God is certain and sure, no matter how long we have to wait for it.

After researching and publishing a two-volume set of over 800 pages on the history of friends of Zion, I realized that there was no home where Christian Zionists of the world could celebrate their history and their heroes. Now, there is the Friends of Zion Heritage Center, the most high-tech, innovative museum in the State of Israel. The Friends of Zion organization is growing on Facebook alone at a rate of 2.3 million a month, and after our first year of operation, has passed the twelve million member mark. It is obvious that Israel's friends are many times greater than her enemies. It's time to focus on those friends, and educate and activate these amazing Christian Zionists.

The late Shimon Peres, Israel's ninth president served as the international chairman of the Friends of Zion Heritage Center. When I shared this vision with him, President Peres said, "I will help you. The reason I will help you is because you want to make friends. It takes so much less energy to make friends than enemies, and to sustain them." He did help us, and took me with him to build that support with a pope (Francis), a president (George W. Bush), and a prince (Albert II of Monaco), each of whom was presented with a Friends of Zion award.

Abraham waited for the promised birth of Isaac for some twenty-five years, but in God's perfect timing, the son of promise was born. When I first met with Prime Minister Menachem Begin more than thirty years ago and we agreed to work together to build a bridge between Christians and Jews, part of that dream was to have a permanent presence in the Holy City. Now we can point to this beautiful facility—a place where we can minister to the Jewish people and to you.

The attitude that pervades Jerusalem Prayer Team partners is one of determination that the Jewish people can now see and hear the stories of Christian Zionists who have provided comfort and aid to them. There is a God-given, biblical—and intimate—connection between Christians and Jews. Based on love and truth, and surrounded by prayer, it can never be broken.

ENDNOTES

1. From *Well with My Soul*, published by Barbour Publishing, Inc. Used by permission, 11.

2. Maria V. G. Havargal, *Memorials of Frances Ridley Havergal* (New York: Anson, D. F. Randolph and Company, 1880), 5.

3. Thomas E. Corts, *Seeking Solace, The Life and Legacy of Horatio G. Spafford* (Birmingham, AL: Sherman Oaks Books, Samford University Press, 2013), 24.

4. Jane Fletcher Geniesse, *American Priestess: The Extraordinary Story of Anna Spafford and the American Colony in Jerusalem* (New York, NY: Doubleday 2008) Kindle Version, Chapter Two.

5. Corts, 29

6. Corts, 30

7. From *Well with My Soul*, published by Barbour Publishing, Inc. Used by permission, 22.

8. Corts, 34

9. Bertha Spafford Vester, *Our Jerusalem: An American Family in the Holy City 1881–1949* (Jerusalem: Ariel Publishing House, 1988), 34.

10. Full Text of *Our Jerusalem*, Bertha Spafford Vester, http://www.archive.org/stream/ourjersalem000091mbp/ourjersalem000091mbp_djvu.txt; accessed August 2016.

11. Vester, 38

12. "The Rescue from the Ville du Harve and the Loch Earn," http://www.catholicprayer.ca/PrayersAnswered/The-Rescue-From-The-Ville-Du-Hav.html; accessed August 2016.

13. https://www.loc.gov/item/mamcol000006; accessed August 2016.

14. Public Domain; words by Horatio Spafford, score by Phillip P. Bliss, 1873; http://www.cyberhymnal.org/htm/i/t/i/itiswell.htm. Note: Phillip Bliss died in a train accident shortly after completing the score.

15. http://www.jameswatkins.com/articles-2/hopeful/itiswell/; accessed July 2016.

16. Al Maxey, "Reflections: Horatio Spafford"; http://www.zianet.com/maxey/reflx331.htl; accessed December 2010.

17. Vester, *Our Jerusalem: An American Family in the Holy City 1881–1949*, 64.

18. "Jaffa," http://www.biblewalks.com/Sites/Jaffa.html; accessed August 2016.

19. Simon Sebag Montefiore, *Jerusalem* (London: Weidenfeld & Nicolson: 2011), 365.

20. Corts, 50-51.

21. Quoted by: Odd Karsten Tveit, *Anna's House: The American Colony in Jerusalem* (Nicosia, Cypress: Rimal Publications, 2011), 79.

22. Vester, *Our Jerusalem: An American Family in the Holy City 1881–1949*, 168.

23. "The American Colony in Jerusalem," http://www.loc.gov/exhibits/americancolony/amcolony-relief.html; accessed August 2016.

24. https://en.wikipedia.org/wiki/Hatikvah; accessed September 2016.

25. Bart Casey, *The Double Life of Laurence Oliphant, Victorian Pilgrim and Prophet* (New York, NY: Post Hill Press, 2015), 6-7.

26. Laurence Oliphant, *Episodes in a Life of Adventure or Moss from a Rolling Stone*, (1887), 23. https://archive.org/stream/episodesinalife00olipgoog#page/n31/mode/2up; accessed September 2016.

27. Laurence Oliphant, *A Journey to Katmandu* (New York, NY: D. Appleton and Company, 1859), 70-71, https://archive.org/stream/journeytokatmand00olipuoft#page/n9/mode/2up; accessed September 2016.

28. Casey, 27

29. Oliphant, *A Journey to Katmandu*, 45

30. Oliphant, *Episodes*, 141

31. http://www.gotquestions.org/Swedenborgianism.html; accessed September 2016.

32. Casey, 97-98

33. Lawrence Oliphant, Letter to John Blackwood, December 10, 1878, quoted in Margaret Oliphant*, *Memoir of the Life of Lawrence Oliphant and of Alice Oliphant, His Wife, Vol. 2* (New York, 1891), 169–170. (*No relation.)

34. Barbara W. Tuchman, *Bible and Sword: England and Palestine from the Bronze Age to Balfour* (New York: Ballatine Press, 1956), 272.

35. The Christadelphians are a small Christian denomination. They might best be described as a conservative Christian movement, which differs from conventional denominations in their beliefs concerning the nature of God, Jesus Christ, the Holy Spirit, and Satan; http://www.religioustolerance.org/chr_delp.htm; accessed January 2011.

36. Laurence Oliphant, *The Land of Gilead* (London: William Blackwood and Sons, 1880), xv-xviii.

37. Oliphant, The Land of Gilead, 294.

38. *Times of London*, January 11, 1882 as quoted by Bart Casey, 213.

39. Margaret Oliphant, *Memoirs*, Vol. II, 215.

40. Ibid, 226.

41. Ibid, 232.

42. Nakdimon Rogel, *The Imber File: In the Footsteps of N. H . Imber in Eretz Israel* (Jerusalem: Mossad Bialik, 1997) 10.

43. Oswald Smith, *Memoir on Laurence Oliphant* (1889), typed transcript, 11; Harris-Oliphant Papers, Columbia.

44. https://en.wikisource.org/wiki/Blackstone_Memorial; accessed September 2016.

45. John F. Walvoord, "Foreword" to William E. Blackstone, *Jesus Is Coming: God's Hope for a Restless World*, 3rd printing of an updated edition, (Grand Rapids, MI: Kregel Publications, 1989), 8.

46. Timothy P. Weber, *On The Road to Armageddon: How Evangelicals Became Israel's Best Friend* (Grand Rapids: Baker Academic, 2004), 102.

47. William E. Blackstone, *Jesus is Coming*, (New York: Fleming Revell, 1908), 162.

48. Ibid., 171, 175.

49. Peter Grose, *Israel in the Mind of America* (New York: Knopf, 1984), 5.

50. William E. Currie, "God's Little Errand Boy."

51. Jerry Klinger, "Christian Zionists Help Make the Jewish State," http://www.jewishmag.com/146mag/brandeis_blackstone/brandeis_blackstone.htm; accessed September 2016.

52. Christian Zionism; http://christianactionforisrael.org/4thcongress2.html. Accessed April 2010.

53. William Eugene Blackstone, "The Blackstone Memorial, 1891," https://en.wikisource.org/wiki/Blackstone_Memorial; accessed September 2016.

54. Ibid.

55. Ibid.

56. The word "Rapture" does not appear in the Holy Bible. The word comes from the Latin "rapturo", a translation of the Greek verb "caught up" found in 1 Thessalonians 4:17.

57. Hilton Obenzinger, "In the Shadow of 'God's Sundial': The Construction of American Christian Zionism and the Blackstone Memorial." Online at: http://www.stanford.edu/group/SHR/5-1/text/obenzinger.html. Last Updated: February 27, 1996. Accessed 2003.

58. Moshe Davis, "Reflections on Harry S. Truman and the State of Israel," in Allen Weinstien and Hoshe Ma'oz (eds.), *Truman and the American Commitment to Israel* (Jerusalem: The Magnes Press, 1981), 83.

59. David Rausch, *Zionism within Early American Fundamentalism, 1878-1918*, (New York: The Edwin Mellen Press, 1979), 269

60. Benjamin Netanyahu, *A Place Among The Nations: Israel and the World* (New York: Bantam, 1993), 16.

61. Grose, *Israel in the Mind of America*, 41.

62. William Blackstone papers, Wheaton College, IL.

63. Melvin I. Urofsky, *A Voice that Spoke for Justine: The Life and Times of Stephen S. Wise* (New York: Albany State University Press, 1982), 147.

64. Weber, On The Road to Armageddon: How Evangelicals Became Israel's Best Friend, 102.

65. David Rausch, The Middle East Maze (Chicago: Moody Press, 1991), 64.

66. Jerry Klinger, "Christian Zionists Help Make the Jewish State," http://www.jewishmag.com/146mag/brandeis_blackstone/brandeis_blackstone.htm; accessed September 2016.

67. Jerry Klinger, "The Messiah and Theodor Herzl," http://www.jewishmag.com/169mag/theodor_herzl_and_messiah/theodor_herzl_and_messiah.htm; accessed September 2016.

68. Carl F. Ehle Jr., "Prolegomena to Christian Zionism in America: The Views of Increase Mather and William E. Blackstone Concerning the Doctrine of the Restoration of Israel," PhD Dissertation at New York University, 1977, 31.

69. Ibid, 41–42.

70. Ibid, 125.

71. Ibid, 125

72. Douglas J. Culver, *Albion and Ariel: British Puritanism and the Birth of Political Zionism* (New York: Peter Lang, 1995), 71–73.

73. Christian Zionism: Definition, *Zionism and Israel—Encyclopedic Dictionary*; http://www.zionism-israel.com/dic/Christian_Zionism.htm; accessed October 2010.

74. Crawford Gribben, *The Puritan Millennium: Literature & Theology, 1550–1682* (Dublin: Four Courts Press, 2000), 46–47.

75. Martha Lou Farmer, "They Believed the Scriptures—the Story of Christian Zionism," *Bridges of Peace*, May 21, 2003, 2.

76. Esther 4:14 nkjv

77. David Rice McKee, "Isaac de la Peyrere: A Precursor of Eighteenth-Century Critical Deists," PMLA Vol. 59, No. 2 (June 1944), 456–485; http://www.jstor.org/discover/10.2307/459339?uid=3739920&uid=2129&uid=2&uid=70&uid=4&uid=3739256&sid=4769884277497; accessed April 2012.

78. "Cromwell and the Jews," http://www.olivercromwell.org/jews.htm

79. Rosemary Radford Ruether and Herman J. Ruether, *The Wrath of Jonah* (Minneapolis: Fortress Press, 2002), 74.

80. James A. Saddington, "Prophecy and Politics: A History of Christian Zionism in the Anglo-American Experience, 1800–1948," PhD Dissertation at Bowling Green State University, 1996, 32.

81. Arnold Dallimore, *Forerunner of the Charismatic Movement: The Life of Edward Irving,* (Edinburgh: Banner of Truth, 1983), 62.

82. Nigel Aston, "Newton, Thomas (1704–1782)," *Oxford Dictionary of National Biography* (Oxford: Oxford University Press, 2004); accessed August 2010.

83. Leon Pinsker, "Auto-Emancipation: An Appeal to His People By a Russian Jew," 1882; http://www.mideastweb.org/autoemancipation.htm; accessed December 2010.

84. Public domain.

85. *The complete Diaries of Theodor Herzl*, Edited by Raphael Patai, translated by Harry Zohn, (Herzl Press, New York, 1960), 312

86. Theodor Herzl to Rev. William Hechler, 16 March 1896, *The Diaries of Theodor Herzl*, edited by Marvin Lowenthal, (Peter Smith Pub.: Gloucester, MA., 1978), 105.

87. Paul C. Merkley, *The Politics of Christian Zionism: 1891–1948* (London: Frank Cass, 1998), 17.

88. Herzl, *The Diaries of Theodor Herzl*, 124–125.

89. Merkley, *The Politics of Christian Zionism: 1891–1948*, 3.

90. *Christian Zionism*; http://mb-soft.com/believe/text/czionism.htm; accessed December 2010.

91. Hermann and Bessi Ellern, "Herzl, Hechler, the Grand Duke of Baden and the German Emperor—1896–1904." Printed in Israel, Published by Ellern's Bank Ltd., Tel Aviv, The Documents have been printed by United Artists Ltd., Tel Aviv and the Text by Goldberg's Press, Jerusalem.

92. Ibid., 6.

93. Harry Zohn, "Herzl, Hechler, the Grand Duke of Baden and the German Emperor," *Herzl Year Book, Vol. 4* (New York: Herzl Press, 1961–62), 210.

94. Harry Zohn, "Herzl, Hechler, the Grand Duke of Baden and the German Emperor," 237.

95. Paul C. Merkley, *The Politics of Christian Zionism*, 16–17.

96. Ibid., 17.

97. Michael J. Pragai, *Faith and Fulfillment*, 271.

98. Paul C. Merkley, *The Politics of Christian Zionism*, 17.

99. Ibid., 23.

100. Rafael Patai, ed., *Encyclopaedia of Zionism and Israel, Volume II* (New York: Herzl Press, 1971), 482.

101. Claude Duvernoy, *The Prince and the Prophet* (Oakville, Ontario, Canada: Christian Action for Israel, 1979), 120.

102. Paul C. Merkley, The Politics of Christian Zionism: 1891–1948, 34.

103. http://www.nytimes.com/learning/general/onthisday/bday/0725.html

104. Barbara Tuchman, *The Proud Tower, A Portrait of Europe Before the War: 1890–1914*, (New York: Ballantine, 1996), 54.

105. Tuchman, *The Proud Tower;* 53.

106. Jerry Klinger, "Beyond Balfour," *The Jerusalem Post*, August 21, 2010, Christian Edition; http://www.jpost.com/ChristianInIsrael/Features/Article.aspx?id=185477; accessed August 2011.

107. Tuchman, *The Proud Tower*, 59.

108. 1911 Encyclopædia Britannica/Balfour, Arthur James, https://en.wikisource.org/wiki/1911_Encyclop%C3%A6dia_Britannica/Balfour,_Arthur_James; accessed October 2016.

109. Balfour, a Leader for Half a Century," *On This Day, The New York Times*, March 20, 1930, Obituaries; http://www.nytimes.com/learning/general/onthisday/bday/0725.html; accessed October 2016.

110. Source, notes of David Hunter Miller, pg 183, Vol I, The Drafting of the Covenant, 1928, Putnam.

111. Balfour, a Leader for Half a Century," *On This Day, The New York Times*, March 20, 1930, Obituaries; http://www.nytimes.com/learning/general/onthisday/bday/0725.html; accessed October 2016.

112. Ibid.

113. Jonathan Schneer, *The Balfour Declaration, The Origins of the Arab-Israeli Conflict* (New York, NY: random House Trade Paperbacks, 2012), 78-79

114. Schneer, 85.

115. Lawrence Davidson, America's Palestine: Popular and Official Perceptions from Balfour to Israeli Statehood (Gainesville, FL: University Press of Florida, 2001), 14.

116. http://history1900s.about.com/cs/holocaust/p/balfourdeclare.htm; accessed October 2016.

117. Phillip Misselwitz and Tim Rieniets, *City of Collision: Jerusalem and the Principles of Conflict Urbanism;* (Germany: Die Deutsche Bibliothek, 2006), 49.

118. Ormsby-Gore's Zionist leanings were developed in Cairo while he was stationed there with the British Arab Bureau. He too had a role in the development of the Balfour Declaration. He was dispatched to Palestine to serve under Dr. Weizmann on the Zionist Commission due, many believe, to his profound grasp of Zionism. In the 1930s, Ormsby-Gore was appointed Colonial Secretary of Palestine during the time when a committee overseen by Lord Robert Peel traveled to Palestine to investigate and make suggestions regarding the British Mandate. Peel and his group ultimately decided it would be better for Palestine to be partitioned. Amid bitter dissention between the Jews and outright rejection from the Arabs, it was shelved.

119. Carroll Quigley, *The Anglo-American Establishment* (New York: Books in Focus, 1981), 169.

120. Schneer, 336.

121. William D. Rubinstein, "The Secret of Leopold Amery," (London: Institute of Historical Research, 2000), 175–196.

122. Shalom Goldman, *Zeal for Zion, Christians, Jews, & the Idea of The Promised Land* (Chapel Hill, NC: The University of North Carolina Press, 2009), 290.

123. Harold Begbie (writing as 'A Gentleman with a Duster'), *Mirrors of Downing Street: Some political reflections,* (London: Mills and Boon,1920), 76–79

124. "Is Lloyd George Israel's Father?," April 20, 2013, http://www.dailypost.co.uk/news/north-wales-news/is-lloyd-george-israels-father-2932875; accessed October 2016.

125. Frank Owen, Tempestuous Journey, Lloyd George His Life and Times (New York, NY: McGraw-Hill Book Company, 1955), 33-34.

126. Abraham Lincoln, memorandum for law lecture, 1850, http://www.notable-quotes.com/l/lawyers_quotes.html; accessed October 2016.

127. Gordon Corrigan, Mud, Blood and Poppycock, (London: Cassell Military Paperbacks, 2003), 309.

128. Robert Lloyd George, *David and Winston* (New York, NY: The Overlook Press, 2008), 258.

129. Robert Lloyd George, 23.

130. Owen, 316.

131. "Lloyd George Says War Will be Fought to the Finish," http://www.rte.ie/centuryireland/index.php/articles/lloyd-george-says-war-will-be-fought-to-the-finish; accessed October 2016.

132. Robert Lloyd George, 175.

133. Kressenstein (1870–1948), a Bavarian-born artillery officer, spent the majority of World War I in the service of the Ottoman Empire. He was appointed military adviser to Djemal Pasha, Fourth Army commander. It was Kressenstein who advocated and disastrously planned the wholly unsuccessful attack on the Suez Canal in January 1915, which opened hostilities on the Palestine Front, damaging Djemal's reputation rather than his own.

134. David Lloyd George, *Memoirs of the Peace Conference* (New Haven, CT: Yale University Press, 1939), 722.

135. Lloyd George, 175.

136. Lawrence Davidson, "Christian Zionism and American Foreign Policy: Paving the Road to Hell in Palestine," *Logos Journal* 4.1, Winter 2005; www.logosjournal.com/issue_4.1/davidson; accessed August 2011.

137. Donald M. Lewis, *The Origins of Christian Zionism: Lord Shaftesbury and Evangelical Support for a Jewish Homeland* (New York: Cambridge University Press, 2010), 5.

138. Leonard Stein, *The Balfour Declaration* (ACLS Humanities eBook, 2008), 6.

139. Owen, 445.

140. Lloyd George and Hitler . . . . Comments on His Visit to Germany and Meeting With Hitler in 1936," *Daily Express*, September 17, 1936; http://www.ww2hc.org/articles/lloyd_george_and_hitler.htm; accessed August 2011.

141. "Norway Debate," *Wikipedia*; http://en.wikipedia.org/wiki/Norway_Debate; accessed August 2011.

142. Ibid.

143. George I. Gay, "Public Relations of the Commission for Relief in Belgium," http://net.lib.byu.edu/estu/wwi/comment/CRB/CRB1-TC.htm; accessed October 2016.

144. http://www.archives.gov/publications/prologue/1989/spring/hoover-belgium.html; accessed June 2012.

145. "World War I: 10th and 20th Forestry Engineers," http://www.foresthistory.org/Research/WWI_ForestryEngineers.htm; accessed October 2016.

146. Walter Clay Lowdermilk, *Conquest of the Land Through 7,000 Years*, https://babel.hathitrust.org/cgi/pt?id=uiug.30112019265732;view=1up;seq=4; accessed October 2016.

147. Pauline Winkler Grey, *The Black Sunday of April 14, 1935, Kansas Historical Society*; http://www.crh.noaa.gov/oun/?n=blacksunday-notes; accessed October 2016.

148. Rory Miller, "Bible and soil: Walter Clay Lowdermilk, the Jordan Valley project and the Palestine debate, https://www.highbeam.com/doc/1G1-102554752.html; accessed October 2016.

149. Moshe Davis, *With Eyes Toward Zion: Scholars Colloquium on America-Holy Land Studies*, (Manchester: Ayer Publishing, 1977), 18.

150. Exodus 33:3, KJV.

151. Menachem Posner, "Why is Israel called the 'Land of Milk and Honey?'" http://www.chabad.org/library/article_cdo/aid/624194/jewish/Why-is-Israel-called-the-land-of-Milk-and-Honey.htm; accessed October 2016.

152. W. C. Lowdermilk, "'TVA' Reclamation Project for the Jordan Valley and a Post-war Solution for the Jewish Refugee Problem," August 10, 1942, *Ben Cohen Papers*, Box 23, Folder 1, Library of Congress, Washington, D.C.

153. Ibid.

154. Walter Clay Lowdermilk, *Palestine: Land of Promise* (London: Victor Gollancz, 1946), 12.

155. Ibid, Dedication.

156. Douglas Helms, "Walter Lowdermilk's Journey: Forester to Land Conservationist," *National Resources Conservation Service*; http://www.nrcs.usda.gov/wps/portal/nrcs/detail/national/about/history/?&cid=nrcs143_021442; accessed September 2016.

157. "Bible and Soil: Walter Clay Lowdermilk, the Jordan Valley Project, and Palestine Debate," https://www.highbeam.com/doc/1G1-102554752.html; accessed September 2016.

158. "Zionist Congresses: The Biltmore Conference," http://www.jewishvirtuallibrary.org/jsource/History/biltmore.html; accessed October 2016.

159. Lowdermilk, 129.

160. Douglas Helms, "Walter Lowdermilk's Journey: Forester to Land Conservationist," *National Resources Conservation Service*; http://www.nrcs.usda.gov/wps/portal/nrcs/detail/national/about/history/?&cid=nrcs143_021442; accessed September 2016. ·

161. http://www.technion.ac.il/technion/agr/general_in/info.html; accessed January 2011.

162. Michael J. Pragai, *Faith and Fulfillment*, 281.

163. Rory Miller, "Bible and soil: Walter Clay Lowdermilk, the Jordan Valley project and the Palestine debate, https://www.highbeam.com/doc/1G1-102554752.html; accessed October 2016.

164. http://www.brainyquote.com/quotes/authors/t/theodor_herzl.html; accessed September 2016.

165. Amos Elon, *Herzl* (New York: Holt, Rinehart and Winston, 1975), 23.

166. Ibid.

167. "The Anti-Semitic Intention of *The Ring of the Nibelung*: An Evaluation of Jewish Culture and Wagner's Dwarven Characters"; http://www.utexas.edu/courses/wagner/selectedessays/pdf/brach.pdf; accessed March 2012.

168. Irwin Abrams, "Alfred Nobel, Bertha von Suttner and the Nobel Peace Prize," Published as "The Odd Couple" in *Scanorama* 23, No. 11, November 1993, 52–56; http://www.irwinabrams.com/articles/oddcouple.html; accessed January 2011.

169. Bertha von Suttner, *Memoirs of Bertha von Suttner: the Records of an Eventful Life* (Boston and London, published for the International School of Peace: Ginn and Company, 1910); www.archive.org/stream/memoirsberthavo00unkngoog/memoirsbertahvo00unkngoog_djvu.txt; accessed December 2010.

170. http://www.jewishvirtuallibrary.org/jsource/judaica/ejud_0002_0013_0_12844.html; accessed October 2016.

171. Reinhold Niebuhr, *The Nation*, February 21, 1942, 215.

172. Herzl, *Der Judenstaat*, cited by C. D. Smith, *Palestine and the Arab-Israeli Conflict*, 4th ed., (New York, NY: Bedford/St. Martins, 2001), 53.

173. Theodor Herzl, *The Diaries of Theodor Herzl*, edited by M. Lowenthal (London: Gollancz, 1958), 11.

174. Ernst Pawel, *The Labyrinth of Exile: A Life of Theodor Herzl* (New York, NY: Farrar Straus Giroux, 1989), 330, and Alex Bein, *Theordor Herzl, A Biography* (Philadelphia, PA: Atheneum, 1945), 229.

175. Montefiore, 374.

176. Ibid, 375.

177. Theodor Herzl, *Theodor Herzl's Tagebücher*, Volume 1 (Berlin, Germany: Judischer Verlag, 1922), 350.

178. N. M. Gelber, *Herzl Year Book*, 124.

179. Ibid., 129–130.

180. Ibid., 131.

181. Ibid., 32.

182. An honor conferred on non-Turkish nationals, it was instituted by Sultan Abdul-Mejid I.

183. Theodor Herzl, *Theodor Herzl's Tagebücher*, Volume 1, 465.

184. Letter from Newlinski to Herzl, January 2, 1897. *Herzl Archive*; accessed February 2010.

185. *Correspondance de l'Est*, No. 212, September 1897; accessed February 2010.

186. Amos Elon, *Herzl*, 400–401.

187. http://www.jewishquotations.com/authors/david-ben-gurion/; accessed October 2016.

188. *Memoirs : David Ben-Gurion* (New York, NY: World Publishing Company, 1970), 36.

189. Michael Bar-Zohar, *Ben-Gurion: A Biography* (Jerusalem: Keter, 1989), 18; translated from Hebrew

190. "Israeli Declaration of Independence," https://en.wikipedia.org/wiki/Israeli_Declaration_of_Independence; accessed October 2016.

191. John Acacia, *Clark Clifford: The Wise Man of Washington* (Lexington, KY: The University Press of Kentucky, 2009), 105.

192. Ambassador Richard Holbrooke, May 2008, *Jerusalem Center for Public Affairs*; http://www.jcpa.org/JCPA/Templates/ShowPage.asp?DRIT=2&DBID=1&LNGID=1&TMID=111&FID=376&PID=0&IID=2203&TTL=President_Truman%E2%80%99s_Decision_to_Recognize_Israel; accessed March 2012.

193. James Pfiffner, *The Modern Presidency* (Florence, KY: Cengage Learning, 2010), 60.

194. David Jeremiah, *What in the World Is Going On?* (Nashville, TN: Thomas Nelson, 2008), 21.

195. Richard H. Curtiss, "Truman Adviser Recalls May 14, 1948, US Decision to Recognize Israel," *Information Clearing House*; http://www.informationclearinghouse.info/article4077.htm; accessed November 2016.

196. "The Recognition of the State of Israel," Truman Library, Eliahu Epstein to Harry S. Truman with attachments re: recognition of Israel, May 14, 1948.

197. Ibid.

198. "The Recognition of the State of Israel," Truman Library, Eliahu Epstein to Harry S. Truman with attachments re: recognition of Israel, May 14, 1948.

199. Arthur A. Goren, *Dissenter in Zion: From the Writings of Judah L. Magnes* (Cambridge, MA: Harvard University Press, 1982), 472.

200. Dylan Thomas, "Do Not Go Gentle Into That Good Night"; http://allpoetry.com/poem/8451903-Do_Not_Go_Gentle_Into_That_Good_Night-by-Dylan_Thomas; accessed November 2016.

201. Shlomo Avineri, "Israel in the Post-Ben-Gurion Era: The Nemesis of Messianiam," *Midstream*, September 1965, 16, 31.

202. Herbert Druks, *John F. Kennedy and Israel* (Westport, CT: Greenwood Publishing Group, 2005), 34.

203. Ibid., 139

204. Avner Cohen, "The Kennedy/Ben-Gurion/Eshkol Nuclear Exchange," *Israel and the Bomb*; http://www.gwu.edu/~nsarchiv/israel/documents/exchange/index.html; accessed October 2016.

205. Georgina Battiscombe, *Shaftesbury, A biography of the Seventh Earl 1801-1885* (London, England: Constable and Company, Ltd, 1974), 3.

206. Geoffrey Best, *Shaftesbury* (London: B. T. Batsford, 1964), 15

207. Lord Shaftesbury, http://www.archive.org/stream/lordshaftesbury00hammuoft/lordshaftesbury00hammuoft_djvu.txt accessed September 2016.

208. Best, 16.

209. Kevin Charles Belmonte, "Greatness Upon Greatness," Christian History Institute, Issue 53, 1997, https://www.christianhistoryinstitute.org/magazine/article/greatness-upon-greatness/; accessed September 2016.

210. http://spartacus-educational.com/IRashley.htm; accessed August 2016.

211. Anthony Ashley Cooper, seventh Earl of Shaftesbury (1801-1885) http://www.victorianweb.org/history/shaftesb.html; accessed September 2016.

212. Battiscombe, 194.

213. http://www.azquotes.com/author/20656-Anthony_Ashley_Cooper_7th_Earl_of_Shaftesbury

214. "Charles Dickens as Social Commentator and Critic," Dr Andrzej Diniejko, D. Litt. in English Literature and Culture, Warsaw University; Contributing Editor, Poland, The Victorian Web, http://www.victorianweb.org/authors/dickens/diniejko.html; accessed September 2016.

215. Stephen Sizer, "John Nelson Darby," *Christian Zionism: Its History, Theology, and Politics*, August 31, 1998, Chapter 4; http://virginiawater.org.uk/christchurch/ (12/13/03).

216. Charles Caldwell Ryrie, *The Basis of the Premillennial Faith* (Neptune, NJ: Loizeaux Brothers, 1953, 1989), 70.

217. Barbara Tuchman, *Bible and Sword*, 75.

218. Ibid, 176.

219. Donald E. Wagner. *Anxious for Armageddon: A Call to Partnership for Middle Eastern and Western Christians* (Scottsdale, PA: Herald Press, 1995), 92. Quoted by John Hubers in "Christian Zionism: A Historical Analysis and Critique."

220. Edwin Hodder, *The Life and Work of the Seventh Earl of Shaftesbury K.G.* (London: Cassel, 1887), Vol. III, 481.

221. Lawrence J. Epstein, *Zion's Call: Christian Contributions to the Origins and Development of Israel* (London: University Press of America, 1984), ix.

MICHAEL DAVID EVANS, the #1 *New York Times* bestselling author, is an award-winning journalist/Middle East analyst. Dr. Evans has appeared on hundreds of network television and radio shows including *Good Morning America, Crossfire* and *Nightline*, and *The Rush Limbaugh Show,* and on Fox Network, *CNN World News,* NBC, ABC, and CBS. His articles have been published in the *Wall Street Journal, USA Today, Washington Times, Jerusalem Post* and newspapers worldwide. More than twenty-five million copies of his books are in print, and he is the award-winning producer of nine documentaries based on his books.

Dr. Evans is considered one of the world's leading experts on Israel and the Middle East, and is one of the most sought-after speakers on that subject. He is the chairman of the board of the ten Boom Holocaust Museum in Haarlem, Holland, and is the founder of Israel's first Christian museum located in the Friends of Zion Heritage Center in Jerusalem.

Dr. Evans has authored a number of books including: *History of Christian Zionism, Showdown with Nuclear Iran, Atomic Iran, The Next Move Beyond Iraq, The Final Move Beyond Iraq,* and *Countdown.* His body of work also includes the novels *Seven Days, GameChanger, The Samson Option, The Four Horsemen, The Locket, Born Again: 1967,* and *The Columbus Code.*

✦ ✦ ✦

Michael David Evans is available to speak or for interviews.

Contact: EVENTS@drmichaeldevans.com.

BOOKS BY: MIKE EVANS

Israel: America's Key to Survival

Save Jerusalem

The Return

Jerusalem D.C.

Purity and Peace of Mind

Who Cries for the Hurting?

Living Fear Free

I Shall Not Want

Let My People Go

Jerusalem Betrayed

Seven Years of Shaking: A Vision

The Nuclear Bomb of Islam

Jerusalem Prophecies

Pray For Peace of Jerusalem

America's War:
The Beginning of the End

The Jerusalem Scroll

The Prayer of David

The Unanswered Prayers of Jesus

God Wrestling

The American Prophecies

Beyond Iraq: The Next Move

The Final Move beyond Iraq

Showdown with Nuclear Iran

Jimmy Carter: The Liberal Left
and World Chaos

Atomic Iran

Cursed

Betrayed

The Light

Corrie's Reflections & Meditations

The Revolution

The Final Generation

Seven Days

The Locket

Persia: The Final Jihad

GAMECHANGER SERIES:

GameChanger

Samson Option

The Four Horsemen

THE PROTOCOLS SERIES:

The Protocols

The Candidate

Jerusalem

The History of Christian Zionism

Countdown

Ten Boom: Betsie, Promise of God

Commanded Blessing

Born Again: 1948

Born Again: 1967

Presidents in Prophecy

Stand with Israel

Prayer, Power and Purpose

Turning Your Pain Into Gain

Christopher Columbus, Secret Jew

Living in the F.O.G.

Finding Favor with God

Finding Favor with Man

Unleashing God's Favor

The Jewish State: The Volunteers

See You in New York

Friends of Zion: Patterson & Wingate

The Columbus Code

The Temple

Satan, You Can't Have My Country!

Satan, You Can't Have Israel!

Lights in the Darkness

The Seven Feasts of Israel

Netanyahu

Jew-Hatred and the Church

The Visionaries

TO PURCHASE, CONTACT: orders@timeworthybooks.
com P. O. BOX 30000, PHOENIX, AZ 85046